LIVING, LOVING, LETTING GO

WHY PEOPLE GET TOGETHER & STAY TOGETHER
AND WHY SOMETIMES IT JUST DOESN'T WORK OUT

LIVING, LOVING, LETTING GO

WHY PEOPLE GET TOGETHER & STAY TOGETHER
AND WHY SOMETIMES IT JUST DOESN'T WORK OUT

Dr. Neal Wiseman

Henschel
HAUS
publishing, inc.
Milwaukee, Wisconsin

Published by
HenschelHAUS Publishing, Inc.
www.henschelHAUSbooks.com

Please contact the publisher for quantity discounts and/
or course adoption.

ISBN: 978159598-691-7
E-ISBN: 978159598-692-4
LCCN: 2018965687

Author photo by Tom Rutherford Photography

*I couldn't have written a book like this without
the support of my wife, Marcy,
and my two children, Rachel and Seth.
I dedicate this book to them with all my love.*

TABLE OF CONTENTS

PREFACE

"**Make a sandwich.**"

"Let me understand, Dr. Wiseman, you want me to make a sandwich?"

"Yes, I would like you to make a husband sandwich. Imagine that you are placing your husband between two pieces of bread. Take a bite. See how it tastes, experience the texture, experience the chewing."

The woman did exactly as I asked. After a few seconds, she screwed up her face.

"What's wrong?" I asked.

"This tastes awful. It's stringy and tough and I just can't swallow it."

"How does this relate to your marriage," I asked.

"It's the same way with my husband. He's really hard to take. I just want to spit him and the marriage out!"

I next heard from the woman about three months later. "I'd like to make an appointment," she told my secretary. "I think I have a lot to talk about."

Over the course of the next several months, we worked on several issues related to disappointment, anger, grieving, and "shame." We discussed the life scripts that she and her husband had written for themselves and the role these scripts played in their "incompatibility."

The hard work, of course, had already been completed: She had made the decision to do something about a marriage that was not working out. In fairness, I should point out that her husband also "made a sandwich" and found her to be "fatty" and "not at all tasty." Both parties amicably accepted the decision to part.

To make wise decisions, suggested Carlos Castaneda, one of our more colorful anthropologists, we need only look to the "path with a heart." Castaneda's advice rings true, but decisions about love relationships are difficult. Searching for the "path with a heart" is troublesome for most, and seemingly impossible for others.

* * *

This book is about people; why they get together, why they stay together, and why sometimes it just doesn't work out. People involved in relationships bring a palette of social and emotional behaviors, attitudes, genetic predispositions, perceptions, and moods into the relationship. Each chapter of *Living, Loving, Letting Go* examines what it takes to create harmonious relationships and why certain behaviors sabotage the attempt.

We begin the book with the cornerstones of love: Passion, Intimacy, and Commitment. We look at the seven signs of a mature love, at the reasons people get together, and what it takes to remain together. We point out the behaviors and the attitudes that destroy relationships, and why couples keep trying despite the pain. We discuss "toxic" personalities, the role of moods, and the creative and destructive power of fantasies and nightmares. We explore the life scripts lovers live and the way these scripts affect the ability to create intimate, passionate and committed relationships. Finally, we describe strategies for dealing with difficult relationships—strategies that require the couple to engage in exercises designed to increase self-awareness and self-discovery-the real healers in our search for "compatibility".

Throughout the book, the reader will find customized scales designed to measure feelings, perceptions and behavior. The scales are important. And they work. In my 35-year practice of psychology, I have used them hundreds of times, and I have always been impressed by how often they help couples understand inner conflict. But they will only work if you spend a few minutes doing what's required.

The payoff is well worth it.

By the end of this book, you will have all the information you need to judge whether the "sandwich" you experience is nourishing you or whether, instead, it is depleting you of energy and happiness.

My wish is that the picture that emerges will lead you to *satori*, a spiritual illumination that brings peace and optimism.

I owe a debt of gratitude to Richard Borofsky and Michael Vincent Miller, Directors of the Boston Gestalt Institute. I borrowed from the writings of Frederick Perls, the "discoverer" and the most charismatic of Gestalt Therapy practitioners, from Barry Stevens and Milton Erickson, and from Ruth Cohn, founder of the Institute for Living/Learning in New York. The writings of Eric Berne and his protégé, Claude Steiner, inspired the life scripts material. Finally, I want to recognize the support of dear friends, Drs. Felix del Vecchio and Bernard Grzyb for their generous offerings of humor and real world savvy.

Neal Wiseman
January 2020

CHAPTER 1

LOVE SONGS

I t's happened to all of us, hasn't it? We meet someone quite extraordinary. We tell our friends, "This is it! This is the person I've been waiting for all my life." Our friends smile and wish us luck.

We continue to date. The courtship is fine: Fancy restaurants, flowers, gentle kisses, and tender caresses. After a few months, we still enjoy the attention we give and we get—at least most of the time. But something is different. We try to understand the minor irritations, the petty arguments, and the differences of opinion. We finally conclude that maybe this isn't the person for whom we've been waiting all our lives.

Sometimes we are certain about who will make us happy, and sometimes we're not. If we happen to stumble upon the right person, no problem: We enjoy the moment, disregard any conflicting realities, and make plans for the future. If our selection definitely is not the right one, again there is no problem. We simply find a way to let him know, accept the disappointment, attempt to part as friends, and learn from the experience.

Sometimes, however, even when we intuitively know the relationship is not going anywhere, we refuse to give up; we make excuses, we procrastinate, we hope things will change.

How can we be sure? After all, we've only known each other for a few months (years). And s/he has become part of our lives: The smell of him, the taste of her, the small gifts and remembrances, the chuckles at an "inside" joke, the smiles at an understanding, secret to the outside world. All the tiny things tug and pull at our waking thoughts like toddlers wanting attention. To rid us of this person now would leave us emptier than we were before; there would be a hole where our heart once was.

Our guides through this process are two people named Ann and Mike. They are typical of the couples who enter into couples therapy. By the time they came for counseling, they had been dating for nearly six months. This was costly in terms of time, money, and personal distress. Mike had been living in England at the time, and he flew to Boston to be with Ann on a monthly basis. As the relationship grew, returning home became increasingly more difficult, Ann often expressing her muted but persistent desire for Mike to remain with her and her children.

Ann and Mike came for couples counseling because they were frightened. Both had been through bad marriages and unsatisfying relationships for many years. They were convinced, they told me, that they were deeply in love. It pained Mike to leave Ann alone. In fact, he had begun to consider leaving his job and moving to Boston so he could be with Ann and her two sons. But both recognized that a decision of this magnitude was a "bit crazy," considering they had only known each other for less than a year. What should they do, they wanted to know. Their fears appeared to be rooted in the uncomfortable feelings of helplessness and loss of control. Each had spent many years alone, independent, and free to make his/her own decisions. Now, as a couple, they needed to develop the kind of interdependency each one had until now tried to avoid. They agreed that at times the tension was so great that despite the fact they felt strongly about each other, they had considered splitting up.

And so began a dozen counseling sessions, Ann and Mike telling me they were at a "crossroad," and that they needed to make a decision about their respective futures.

It wasn't that they weren't in love, they assured me. "We don't really know what the problem is, but it needs to be resolved quickly," Ann said within the first ten minutes of the session. We were to spend several months tracking down the problems, the doubts, the fears, and the insecurities, and in the process Ann and Mike learned all about who they were and what they wanted from each other.

Ann

Ann's two failed marriages seemed to be the direct result of early decisions. The decisions were based on the (unconscious) messages passed along to her by her mother who showed her "how" to reach certain goals, and inadvertently reinforced by her father who showed her "what" goals were worth achieving. Ann decided at the age of nine years she would prefer to be a good wife and mother rather than to be a career woman, although she knew she was brighter and more competent than either of her husbands. She learned how to be a good mother from her mother. Ann's father rewarded his daughter and his wife with generous praise and appreciation.

Ann's childhood was relatively happy; her parents demonstrated love, care, and thoughtfulness. But they neglected to teach her the importance of anger. Without instruction in the proper use of anger, Ann became vulnerable to the whims and unreasonable demands of her spouses.

To help her cope with feelings of helplessness, Ann identified with TV actresses. She began to emulate the actress' attitudes and behavior. They became her mythical heroines, the people who could best help Ann develop a life script into which her values—the do's and don'ts of life—could be incorporated. She was particularly drawn to the good/patient/spiritually enlightened types of women's roles.

As a result, Ann spent most of her time caring for her family. She was always prepared to set an extra place at the dinner table on five minutes notice. She drove her children to school, took her husbands' laundry to the cleaners, went to the Little League games and, with the little energy left over, she prepared meals and kept the social calendar.

She often felt neglected and ignored. Deep down she hungered for the attention her husbands generally reserved for clients and friends. Her resentment grew, but it was never voiced; after all, she reasoned, this was what being a good mother and wife was all about. Halfway through each of her marriages, Ann began to develop periods of fatigue and depression. She began to binge eat and, at one point, gained nearly thirty pounds.

She was unhappy and she was lonely. She wanted to be acknowledged as something more than a servant. When her family tried to escape the barrage of complaints, Ann created feelings of guilt subsequently leading to anger on the part of the family and withdrawal on the part of Ann. The unhappiness took its toll: Ann developed a list of "illnesses" and complaints that her family finally couldn't ignore. Ann's inability to express her anger directly and effectively ultimately drained her of joy and spontaneity. When her husbands wanted to enjoy physical closeness, Ann became "frigid," a covert attempt to punish them for their lack of attention and warmth. In moments of despair, she wondered why she was not respected or appreciated by her family; she was always so "nice," "sacrificed everything for her family," and "never got angry."

Her seething resentment had begun to alienate friends and family alike. She began to feel used and cheated, and she had seriously entertained the idea of suicide, all the while chauffeuring the kids from game to game and setting an extra place at mealtime for her husbands' cronies.

About six months before she and Mike came to see me, Ann had gone to England to present a paper at a convention. As a writer, she was interested in the plight of mature women who had experienced what she had experienced. The paper she presented discussed the changing language of romance, the use of specific "romantic" words to stimulate and provoke feelings and thoughts. Her paper was well received.

After the applause had subsided, Mike approached her. He had come to hear her speak because even in London, where he was then living, he'd read her books and thought she had a wonderful sense of humor. He'd owed it to himself, he said, to meet her at this conference. Had he known how beautiful she was, he told her, he would have thought of some way of meeting her even earlier.

At first Ann couldn't accept Mike's flattery. It felt uncomfortable, she said, "rather like an ill-fitting suit." She had to admit, though, that

Mike's attention did stir up old memories and feelings she'd buried after her divorce two years before. She also had to admit that these stirrings scared her to death: She wanted to run, to get away quickly before—and she knew it would happen—the gentleman's flattery dissolved the defenses she had worked so hard to erect.

After her second divorce, Ann abandoned the search for male companionship, investing her energies instead in her family and her work. She had reconciled herself to a life of celibacy and service. Now her resolve was melting, and she was rediscovering the feelings of passion and desire she had suppressed long ago. Here with this man, with this stranger, she suddenly felt weak and vulnerable. She was confused, powerless, and worst of all, she knew that if he had asked her to extend her visit, she would have done so without hesitation.

Mike

As we worked together, a picture of the couple's needs and desires emerged. Mike, of course, had developed his own life script as a youngster. At the age of fourteen he had put all the pieces together and decided academic achievement and the pursuit of intellectual matters were priorities in his life. His father had also been an "intellectual" who emphasized the usefulness of the rational mind. He let Mike know through his attitudes and behavior that feelings were to be discounted, his father observing that emotions produced discomfort in some cases, and a complete loss of control in others.

Mike learned his lessons well. He always "used his head," as his mother was fond of telling her friends. His heroes included Albert Einstein and Bertrand Russell; however, he was never able to emulate their ability to balance intellect with emotion. His favorite book was *Twenty-Thousand Leagues Under the Sea*, and when he wasn't busy "using his head," he was thinking about improbable but heady futuristic thoughts. Ultimately, Mike became emotionally detached, but financially successful. He became a corporate lawyer, earning more money in a single year than his father had earned in a lifetime.

Unfortunately, the emphasis on rational thought and logic had robbed him of the opportunity to experience love and warmth. He felt empty and incomplete as a man. His only marriage failed largely as a result of his choosing as a bride a woman even more rational and more detached than he was. The two spent many hours planning the relationship and figuring out how best to meet their financial and social needs. Somehow, it never worked out. Neither could satisfy the submerged but powerful need for intimacy and closeness. After several years of frustration, they parted amiably, noting that the "spark" simply wasn't there.

As Mike grew up, he began to feel "ugly inside." He had always sensed there was something "missing" in his life. However, the vocabulary of the rational view did not include concepts such as warmth, self-sacrifice, and compassion, and therefore he couldn't identify the problem. His early decisions about life hadn't allowed him to accept the kindness of others, or, perhaps more importantly, to fully trust what others told him.

With the death of his father, the support for Mike's script weakened. Mike began to reread Einstein and Russell. He began to question why his marriage failed. He was able to better understand that, unless he could balance his intellect with compassion and spontaneity, there could be little happiness in a relationship. This insight prompted him to consider the possibility of an alternative approach to life. The result of this decision was a spiritual pilgrimage, which took him to Tibet, the Ashrams of Colorado and the Encounter Groups of Esalen at Big Sur in California. He had been home merely two weeks when he heard about the convention Ann was to attend and decided it was time to try out some of the new thinking he'd picked up along the way.

The truth was that Ann and Mike had been searching for the right combination of passion, intimacy, and commitment for years. They'd begun the search for happiness even before their divorces were finalized.

Our first session took place when the couple had been dating for about six months. They wanted to know whether there was a way to "make sure that their love would last." There was of course no way to guarantee the durability of their relationship. Still, they needed to learn what coupling was all about, and we set out to do exactly that.

Chapter 2
The Three Stages of Coupling

T he course of treatment went smoothly. After listening to their concerns, I presented the young couple with a series of concepts and exercises that I thought might provide them with insight into the nature of their difficulties. Mike decided not to relocate until he and Ann could make the necessary decisions, but he did take a sabbatical from work and temporarily moved into a small apartment in Cambridge. And we began to work. We reviewed the history of their relationship, and discussed some of the ingredients of successful relationships and "love" as we in the industrialized nations use that term.

Passion, intimacy, and commitment are the three dimensions of what we commonly call love, and once we meet someone special, we spend many of our waking hours (and sleeping hours as well!) thinking about love and how it feels. Our success ultimately depends on our ability to negotiate the three stages of coupling:

Stage I: Initial Contact

The first stage, the initial contact, involves hedonistic pleasure and the excitement of the senses. We become fascinated (fastenated). A certain look, the sound of the voice, the agility of a movement, the touch of the skin, the taste of the lips, the smell of the hair become a complex package of sensations that lead most often to an overwhelming feeling of sexiness. When this feeling develops into a "caring," expressed as unselfish giving and the full acceptance of pleasure, we are well on our way to love, the feeling that transcends the senses and knocks at the door of a mature awareness of intimacy, commitment, and passion.

We often experience the contact stage as "madness." (In the middle ages marrying out of a sense of love was outlawed for noblemen because—so the thinking went—their judgment would become so impaired that they could put the family wealth at risk.) The primary feeling is infatuation, commonly a one-way affair that requires no real love-partner. The object of our attention smites us with a smile; we consume him with our entire being. There is no reality during this phase of t(w)ogetherness. Our lover is a fantasy; he doesn't exist in actuality, but we refuse to believe it. Often the object of our desires has no idea that he has precipitated a state of excitement so overwhelming that his mere presence keeps loins and minds boiling over in erotic fantasies and happily-ever-after endings.

Sometimes the Mikes and Anns of our lives become equally fascinated. Fantasies beget fantasies. Today we are only teenagers, but tomorrow, with the help of our lover, we shall be kings or queens, warriors of great causes, homeowners, mothers or fathers of 2.3 bright children, and a 50 percent shareholder in the greatest love affair that ever was. The results, of course, can often be tragic: early marriage for the innocent or the unprepared, along with the attendant burdens of children, creditors, and an early divorce with its grief, its subsequent disappointment, and its cynicism.

Stage II: Falling in Love

If we survive confrontation and/or sexual contact with our lover, we might be lucky enough to enter Stage II, falling in love. Our perceptions become distorted to varying degrees; our judgment is often based on our wishes and fears rather than on the dictates of reality. The true nature of the relationship is not yet clear. Nonetheless, we feel connected.

With this connection, we develop an alliance and interdependency. We become protective, jealous, and perhaps possessive. We begin to build a repertoire of excuses and distortions to help us understand our lover and to rationalize his behavior. Our alcoholic lover is not really an alcoholic; he is simply a frog that needs to be kissed by the beautiful princess. Our psychotic lover is not really out of her mind; she simply needs understanding. The psychopath, without a shred of conscience, doesn't really want to be abusive or cruel; he just had a bad home life, etc. The blind lead the blind.

For most people, fortunately, the sifting and lifting process works out well. With time, the relationship becomes tested and retested. What is acceptable is separated from what isn't acceptable. If the object of our fascination isn't exactly our cup of tea, we either eliminate him from future dreams or, if we are exceptionally tactful, we part as friends. If we deny the discomfort of our relationship, however, and forge a marriage or some other kind of committed relationship, we can expect much tension, emotional withdrawal, anger, or feelings of betrayal.

Stage III: Being in Love, Coupling

If, however, we survive the confrontation with our passion and our vulnerability, we proceed on to the next phase of the experience—that of being in love, of coupling. This particular stage in the process is no less fraught with danger. While the relationship has passed a series of tests, most often it has not yet been galvanized by the passage of time.

Trust comes into play. Are we willing to suspend judgment and to become vulnerable? Doubts and fears remain, but we are determined to please (and to be pleased by) our partner. We learn how to ask for what we need as an equal in the relationship. Often, we are disappointed, and the pain is great: we sometimes feel misunderstood and confused. We discover that what we think is real isn't real at all—that our partner isn't really a father, a mother, a sister, or a brother. Emotions flow freely. Sometimes we feel we give too much and get too little or, conversely, we get too much and give too little.

Nonetheless, we can still look at our prince/ss with kindness and caring. The bad times may bring us to a point of despair, but the good times give us a sense of fulfillment. We are oxen under the same yoke, and marriage, the little house with the white picket fence, and the 2.3 bright children, become real possibilities.

Falling in love (connecting) and being in love (coupling) are different. The difference lies in the impact of time and experience. While the quality and intensity of the relationship may not differ, there is nonetheless a ripening, a maturing of the process of being together. Subtle changes appear in the way we interact with, and the way we perceive the person who has finally made it through the layers of our doubts, and the filters of our desires.

CHAPTER 3
THE SEVEN SIGNS OF LOVE

As our sessions proceeded, Ann and Mike became more relaxed. Their fears had not yet subsided, but they seemed to be able to view their concerns more objectively. At one point, Ann said, "I know we really love each other, but how do we know for sure? I may be old-fashioned, but I'm from Missouri and need to be shown."

Part of the problem was that Ann was unsure of her judgments—at least when it came to men and romance. She was looking for a guarantee, and no guarantees were forthcoming. Nonetheless, I completely agreed with her: she really did need to be "shown." But, I wondered, could she recognize it even if she were shown? It was time to discuss the signs of love.

Culture has always defined what we mean by love. In Medieval societies, the aristocracy valued wealth far more than it valued romance. In the Middle East, happy marriages have centered around the ability of the woman to produce heirs. In aboriginal cultures, the hunting ability and physical prowess of the man are major considerations. In industrialized nations, however, romantic love seems to be the preferred kind of love, and it has several characteristics:

1. Shared physical and emotional boundaries: We want exclusive companionship with our partner. We experience a sense of loss and a sense of emptiness when we are apart. The concept of being a couple encompasses both mind and body. At night there is a yearning to retreat into each other's arms, locked in an embrace of caring. The difference in our values becomes more tolerable as we take on our lover's perception of reality. Our boundaries might become fused (and often con-fused). Souls and minds join until we feel part of, yet separate from, each other.

2. Communication: We want to share our feelings, our thoughts, and our experiences, and us. Verbal communication, we learn, is only one way to get the message across. We discover that too much talk can disrupt the easy flow of feelings between two people in the successful coupling mode. Rather than becoming the bridge between two worlds, words become a wall that separates and keeps our worlds apart. A gentle look, a kindness, a small, unexpected gift, a card on an unbirthday—all these often mean much more than talk.

3. Seesaw Affection: Part of the maturation process is discovering the balance between giving and taking. If the balance is skewed so that one party is always the "giver" and the other is always the "taker," the relationship will also be skewed. Givers often play the more aggressive role and, still more often, end up feeling deprived, because their kindness will never be fully returned. Takers, on the other hand, become passive and subordinate in the relationship, a position that frequently leads to a feeling of resentment.

The "seesaw" refers to acts of reciprocation. We give and take according to our need, our energy, our generosity, and our assertiveness. If one side of the see-saw is always heavier than the other, the play becomes tedious and, even worse, boring. Most of us, miraculously, if we are truly in love, learn how and when to give affection freely and how and when to accept it freely. A mature relationship cannot survive without this sense of balance.

4. Trust: With the increase in intimacy and commitment, there is an increase in trust. During the "falling in love" stage, we test the waters and learn what we can expect from a relationship. If the evolutionary forces are working properly, the "bad" matches are weeded out and those that remain will, at least in theory, lead to mutual trust, a sense of loyalty, and faith that all problems will work themselves out. Goodwill and benevolence flow abundantly and carry the relationship into the future. We open ourselves up, making us vulnerable to hurt and disappointment, guided only by the unshakable notion that Mr. Right would never deliberately do anything to harm us.

Invariably our vulnerability is tested. Our soul mate partner fails a particular test: a birthday is forgotten, a tiny embarrassment in front of guests, a temper outburst when we've done something silly. If the pain of the disappointment is circumstantial, if it is not the product of malevolence, the emotional wounds heal, and the essential goodness of the relationship is reinforced.

Once the covenant of trust has been broken because of deliberate cruelty or abuse, however, the potential for hurt hangs over the relationship like the Sword of Damocles; the very essence of our love is negated, and we become profoundly unhappy. The strain, the anger, and the pain infiltrate all aspects of our feelings of togetherness. Worst of all, we feel something akin to shame, a feeling that diminishes the likelihood that the situation can ever be entirely rectified.

Shame and accompanying feelings of humiliation need to be considered in terms of the "existential" positions of the parties involved. "Existential" in this case means the very essence of our relationship, not only with people but with life itself. If we learn at an early (preverbal) age to think of ourselves as inferior (small, ugly, stupid, worthless, unacceptable), our vulnerability is very great indeed. Ironically, so is our willingness to forgive those who hurt us, because at a deep level we feel we deserve the abuse and the pain.

Our lover also might be willing to tolerate more than is healthy, because disappointment is consistent with the picture he has developed of himself over the years. Consistency neutralizes the act of cruelty.

If either our lover and/or we think poorly of ourselves, if we have low self-esteem because of either real or imagined rejection by our earliest caretakers, there is a better than even chance that our relationship will never ripen fully, although we might pretend otherwise. Often, we will kiss and make up, only to be deluged with not-always conscious feelings of suspiciousness, helplessness, and rage, followed in short order by the re-entry into the "what's next" emotional lottery we've come to expect.

5. Hold Me Tight/Let Me Loose: The exchange of affection between two people goes hand in hand with the need to establish a balance between possessiveness and tolerance. Possessiveness is born of the universal need to enjoy the exclusive rights to our lover's mind and body. Tolerance involves an acceptance of him as a being separate from us, a being with a life of his own.

Along with passion and intimacy comes the feeling of ownership, a feeling that he'll be there for us as long as we want him to be. The adult part of us does not always enjoy the idea of "owning" someone, an idea that seems to sneak into the bedroom like an unwanted guest. However, the child in us—the part of us that is insecure and uncertain—wants our partner to spend his energy and his time with us. His time is our time; his energy is our energy.

Work, hobbies, pastimes, friends, relatives, and sometimes— perhaps more often than we would like to admit—even the children become rivals for the attention we have come to believe properly belongs to us. When the time, the energy, and the affection are not forthcoming, we often become mildly resentful, mildly jealous, mildly suspicious, and mildly sad.

This possessive attitude is not entirely without benefit: when it is applied realistically, we enjoy the exclusivity of the relationship, because, after all, exclusivity is the very essence of being coupled.

The Hold Me Tight/Let Me Loose phenomenon exerts a powerful influence on the quality of the connection between two people. Its influence, however, is directly related to the degree to which the attendant feelings are acknowledged and accepted. Too much of one and not enough of the other leads to a disruptive and maddening search for the proper emotional balance. We begin to vacillate between holding on too tight and letting go too much, overshooting the mark, retracting blurted-out comments, recanting legitimately held positions, always trying to re-synchronize the emotional seesaw.

The man says, "Hold Me Tight" while making love, and "Let Me Loose" shortly thereafter, often feeling guilty that he has given too much of his passion and not enough of his compassion during the act. The woman says, "Hold Me Tight" while making love and "Keep Holding Me Tight" until I have to fix my hair in the morning, then "Let Me Loose" (that is, no hanky-panky until I feel pretty again), often feeling bitchy and demanding. The man says, "Hold Me Tight" (rub my back, fix me a drink, tell me how smart I am, etc.) when he has had a tough day at work but "Let Me Loose" to go bowling with his buddies. The woman says "Hold Me Tight" (hold my hand, tell me you love me, tell me how pretty I am, etc.) on the dance floor, but "Let Me Loose" (give me time alone with my friends, don't call me too much at work, etc.) when she wants to maintain a sense of independence and self-sufficiency.

The exchanges may be harsh or gentle, spirited or subdued, but they are always designed to establish a harmonious beat to our dancing souls. If we are basically healthy and have developed an optimistic existential position, equilibrium will be reached. We'll begin to recognize when to hold on and when to let loose. Shared moments will be nurturing and uplifting.

If, on the other hand, after much effort, the Hold Me Tight/Let Me Loose seesaw cannot be balanced, something is very much wrong with the connection, and the coupling process will not proceed.

A certain degree of possessiveness and a mild annoyance with prolonged separation generally are positive signs that the tree of love has borne palatable fruit. Battling is part of loving; when it replaces it, however, it is time to cash in our chips and look elsewhere.

6. Protectiveness and Self-sacrifice: The willingness to ensure our lover's safety and comfort to a greater degree than our own is a universal sign of a ripened relationship. The emotional climate is one of total spiritual giving, of transcending our own financial, physical, and emotional welfare for the sake of our partner's. The fact that our partner, if the partnership is an equal one, also develops a self-sacrificing attitude, prevents a lopsided altruism, an unhealthy one-way relationship that leads to feelings of being cheated or, in more serious cases, a blatant masochistic involvement.

7. Sex: Many articles have been written about (1) the all-consuming importance of sex and (2) the "myth" that sex is important at all. The truth, of course, is a bit more complicated. If the sexual act is an act of passion rather than an act of release, then sex is indeed one dimension of a three-dimensional love. As such, a fully matured love won't—with certain exceptions—blossom until there is a union of bodies and souls.

The self-sacrificing quality of a loving relationship, except in cases where one of the partners has a severe disability, requires that we offer our sexual selves completely and that our partner reciprocate. A great part of this is simple biology; a greater part is the desire to please, to be pleased, and then to merge as one being.

Couples who have demonstrated their devotion through self-sacrifice, sharing, tolerance, and healthy feelings of possessiveness might be able to survive and grow without much sexual contact. A majority of couples, however, need regular, consistent, and tender sexual attention in order to make the relationship complete. Sadly, the excuses used to avoid physical closeness have become so widely accepted that they have taken on a comic flavor.

The "Not tonight, honey, I've got a headache," the "I'm tired," and the "Children will hear" clichés are bandied about bedrooms, day and night. There is a game-like quality to the transaction, totally predictable in sequence and outcome: first there is a subtle suggestion, then a harsher demand; the other party feigns illness or fatigue. We go to bed angry, frustrated, and confused.

If there is goodwill, we will experience a night of fitful sleep and, in the morning, acknowledge destructive, and perhaps dishonest, gamesmanship. If we are mature enough to discuss the problem openly and courageously, we will kiss and make up. Mature love and caring demand it.

If the healthy resolution has eluded us, there will be many months and years of quiet irritability and ugliness. We will become grouchy and querulous, all the time trying to balance the seesaw, but to no avail. The game will renew itself the next night and the next year: the same beginning to the story, the same middle, and the same ending.

Abstinence for extended periods of time, that is, until someone begins to feel deprived, is a sign of serious difficulties with the coupling process, protestations notwithstanding. On the other hand, there are relationships that have none of the qualities of love except for high sexual activity. Such a one-dimensional love is two dimensions short of completion. As we advance in years, and commitment and intimacy play more significant roles in our lives, a passion/sex-only relationship will leave us battling low self-esteem for the next twenty or thirty years of our lives.

Ninety percent of the time, enjoyable, spontaneous, and tender sex on a regular basis, combined with feelings of intimacy and commitment, is the litmus test of a relationship. At any given time, we need only to assess the quality of our loving to determine the quality of our love.

What is interesting about these seven qualities is that they cannot simply be categorized into any single one of the three dimensions of love: commitment, passion, or intimacy. Each quality fits into all three dimensions to varying degrees. Trust, for example, plays a predominant role in Intimacy but certainly is also required for Commitment and Passion. Likewise, Hold Me Tight/Let Me Loose requires a broad understanding that our partner will be there the next day, that is, that he is committed, that there is a powerful element of passion involved.

When Ann and Mike finally met away from the crowded hall, they found themselves treading the waters of passion, testing and re-testing, checking and re-checking, to determine whether each could endure the lag time between attraction and intimacy, between infatuation and commitment. What is important is to realize that, by the time they had met each other, a selection process had already been at work. Both shared an interest in writing, and both were ready to respond to the signals from an interested party.

Their contact was sharp: their eyes met, and a thunderbolt of passion triggered erotic fantasies. After they explored common interests, they continued to be attracted to each other, and courtship and physical contact followed.

Along with the more subtle adjustment to each other's needs and desires, they had matched and sorted experiences in an attempt to make the major pieces of life—religion, desire for children, politics, values—fit together without too much strain. Enough pieces came together, and they discovered enough passion to glue the pieces in place. Ann and Mike—most likely without conscious knowledge of it—progressed from the "falling in love" phase to the "being in love" phase.

Time was most important at that point because, as with everything else in life, they needed time to determine whether the mortar keeping the pieces together was strong enough. Clearly, Ann and Mike had discovered strange and wonderful but not always comfortable feelings developing inside them. They had discovered the need for physical and emotional closeness, the need to share, the tendency to feel jealous, and the desire to sacrifice their happiness to ensure their lover's happiness.

These feelings were not mutually exclusive. One did not preclude the other. Rather, the coupling process involved a number of processes occurring simultaneously. Keeping track of each one was difficult if not impossible. Nonetheless, it was possible to know whether things were really working out: Ann and Mike simply added the desire to go to bed with each other at night to the desire to wake up and face the world with each other in the morning. The sum of the equation should have left them feeling happy, fulfilled, and mildly euphoric. Anything less would have meant that they'd kidded themselves into complacency.

Ann and Mike were lucky. Waking up next to each other in the morning was an exhilarating experience for both of them. For many of us, however, the chances of finding a partner who inspires feelings of passion, commitment, and intimacy are relatively remote; and for virtually all of us, the task of sifting through possible candidates for our romantic attentions is daunting.

Yet we continue to take risks, dating someone less than perfect, rationalizing our own intuitive sense of discomfort, in the attempt to find someone who matches our emotional, sexual, and intellectual needs. More often than not we finally succeed, but not without the oftentimes excruciating pain of having to terminate one relationship after another until we are once again able to regain the sense of balance we may have lost during an unsuccessful coupling effort. Ann went through two divorces and many romantic entanglements before she finally withdrew from the fray to restore her sense of dignity and self-esteem. When she chose to entertain thoughts about Mike, she was ready to take another chance on yet another man.

Ending an affair of the heart can be a wretched and wrenching experience. The stronger the glue holding the relationship together, the more difficult it is. Couples who have spent time getting to know one another, who have become intimately acquainted with tiny bits of behavior—what makes each other giggle and respond sexually or smile knowingly—who have committed themselves to thoughts of a future with children and grandchildren have a very difficult time indeed. Yet, the de-structuring (destruction) of the relationship might be as necessary as life itself.

CHAPTER 4

COMPATIBILITY

"We're in love, but are we compatible?"

Ann's comfort level had increased since our first session. She was experiencing all the signs of love, she told me. Mike agreed that he too had been experiencing all the feelings that people who were really in love seem to experience.

"Well," I said, "it seems like the two of you are ready to make your decision."

"I'm not sure we are," responded Mike. "We've always known that we were in love, but are we really compatible?"

It was becoming clear to me that Ann and Mike had a lot more to deal with than just indecisiveness. I wasn't sure at this point whether any answer I could give them would satisfy their need for certainty. Nonetheless, Mike's point was well taken. Are couples who are in love necessarily compatible?

The answer is: It depends.

We tend to (con)fuse "love" with a momentary passion, an intense experience of intimacy, or a vow of commitment. Love, however, is three-dimensional; while any one of the three dimensions, in its pure state, may be interpreted as "love," rarely does a relationship develop into a durable and satisfying coupling without the qualities of all three dimensions. The passion-intimacy-commitment triad produces many combinations, and some combinations produce greater happiness for some couples than for others. After I briefly described the three dimensions of love to Ann and Mike, they agreed to complete the Compatibility Scale. (Detailed descriptions of the three dimensions are presented in following three chapters.)

The Three Dimensions of Love: Intimacy, Passion, and Commitment

The *Intimacy dimension* is characterized by a best-friend relationship with your lover. You share interests (hobbies, pastimes, religion, politics), and thoughtfulness and warmth appear to be more important than the sizzling passion so often described in romance novels. You tend to reveal yourself slowly and gradually. The relationship's security is based on freely shared feelings and experiences, caring and nurturing, and an equal partnership at all levels.

The *Passion dimension*, on the other hand, is intense and often short-lived. Devotion alternates with jealousy and insecurity; and emotional peaks and valleys occur with regularity. You and your lover experience high sexual energy. Nonetheless, despite your lover's declarations of love and adoration, you often need reassurance. There tends to be a belief in love at first sight and mystical symbolism. Your energy level is high; you crave excitement, and value physical attributes (beauty, strength, agility). Planning for the near future is more common than planning for the distant future. High Passion couples also tend to disclose inner drives, fears, desires, and strivings soon after first meeting in contrast to high-intimacy couples who reveal themselves slowly.

The third dimension is *Commitment*. Couples with a high degree of commitment generally value self-sacrifice, forgiveness of transgressions, and consistent support during times of adversity. Planning includes long-range goals, and the relationship is based on patience and "being there" rather than passion or self-disclosure.

At the end of our fourth session, I handed Ann and Mike the Compatibility Scale. Their responses revealed feelings and attitudes that neither one could have appreciated before their great search for the "path with a heart." Here is the scale as I presented it to them:

"The Compatibility Scale below is designed to help couples discover attitudes, beliefs, and feelings about their partners. To complete the scale, simply rate the degree to which you agree with each statement by writing your rating on the line next to each statement. For example, in the column for item #1, you might rate "I believe in love at first sight" a "5" (Strongly Agree). In like fashion, complete the ratings for all thirty items.

After you have completed all the ratings, add up the numbers and interpret the total scores as instructed at the end of the exercise. The results will reveal how you perceive intimacy / passion / commitment—the three dimensions of love. The results also will give you a "compatibility profile" that might assist you in deciding whether you want to continue or terminate your relationship. Use the following code as a guide:

1 = Strongly Disagree, Not at All
2 = Disagree, Seldom
3 = About Average, As Much as Most People
4 = Agree, Often
5 = Strongly Agree, Always
? = Don't know enough to rate this item

Item		Rating
1P	I believe in "love at first sight."	_____
2P	Sometimes I want to be with my lover all the time.	_____
3I	My lover and I share feelings and thoughts more than most other couples.	_____
4I	My lover and I feel so emotionally close that we feel and think like one person.	_____
5I	I trust my lover enough to be vulnerable.	_____
6P	I hate to admit it, but at times I feel overly possessive of my lover.	_____
7P	I love my lover so much that I am willing to sacrifice everything I own to make him / her safe and happy.	_____

8C   I often think about how my lover and I will look and feel together ten years from now. _____

9I   I feel my affection is fully reciprocated by my lover. _____

10P   My lover is the most sexually attractive person I know. _____

11I   What I like best about my sexual relationship with my lover is the tenderness. _____

12C   I can't think of anything I would rather do than spend the rest of my life with my lover by my side. _____

13P   I believe my lover will be just as sexually attractive to me in ten years as s/he is right now. _____

14I   Nothing makes me happier than pleasing my lover. _____

15I   I didn't realize I was in love until I had known my lover for many months. _____

16P   The first time I met my lover I felt I wanted to reveal everything about myself. _____

17C   I am ready to commit myself to this relationship right now. _____

18C   I'm happy just spending time with my lover. _____

19C   I feel more secure knowing that my lover will be with me when things get tough. _____

20I   Friendship is more important than sex and romance. _____

21C   The most important part of any relationship is total commitment. _____

22P   The first time we kissed I felt sexy all over. _____

23P   Sometimes I get so excited just thinking about my lover that I have trouble falling asleep at night. _____

24I   Talking and listening are often more important in a relationship than making love. _____

25C   Even though sometimes I don't really feel "in love," I will always be there when my lover needs me. _____

26P   I would rather suffer than watch my lover suffer. _____

27C   I would not be willing to marry (again) unless I knew for sure it would last a lifetime. _____

28I Whatever I own is for my lover to do with as (s)he pleases. _____
29C The best relationships are the ones that last the longest. _____
30C "Until death do us part" is the most important part of
       the wedding vow.   _____

The Compatibility Profile

To determine your compatibility profile, transfer the ratings from the Compatibility Scale above to the appropriate spaces below and add up the ratings for each of the columns as indicated:

PASSION		INTIMACY		COMMITMENT	
Item	Rating	Item	Rating	Item	Rating
1P	_____	3I	_____	8C	_____
2P	_____	4I	_____	12C	_____
6P	_____	5I	_____	17C	_____
7P	_____	9I	_____	18C	_____
10P	_____	11I	_____	19C	_____
13P	_____	14I	_____	21C	_____
16P	_____	15I	_____	25C	_____
22P	_____	20I	_____	27C	_____
23P	_____	24I	_____	29C	_____
26P	_____	28I	_____	30C	_____
Total P _____		Total I _____		Total C _____	

On any given dimension, scores between 34 and 50 are High (H), scores between 25 and 33 are Average (A), and scores between 10 and 24 are considered Low (L). (Please note: five or more "?" suggests that you don't know each other well enough to complete the scale.)

Interpretations

Certain styles of loving are more compatible than others. High Commitment ratings, for instance, are most compatible with other styles because it often assures consistency and availability. A Low Intimacy relationship, on the other hand, would seem to be difficult to tolerate in all but the most superficial relationships although some survive when there is enough Passion and Commitment.

While not commonplace, highly "incompatible" relationships do occur with surprising regularity and sometimes endure year after year. While we cannot say with certainty who will mix well with whom, what we can do is "bet the odds." The odds favor the compatible relationships and, clearly, do not favor the "mismatches." Below are the three most compatible and the four least compatible combinations.

The Most Compatible Combinations

Combination #1: Both members of the couple have High Passion, at least Average Intimacy and High Commitment

High sexual energy, the desire to be with your lover, and the willingness to endure hardships make this a winning combination, although the relative lack of self-revelation, as indicated by an average score on the Intimacy scale, will leave one of the partners always wondering, "What is he really thinking?"

Combination #2: Both people have at least Average Passion and High Intimacy and High Commitment

Nurturing feelings toward your lover and a commitment for life are more important than passion, excitement, or sexual contact. You share thoughts, interests, and a strong friendship, as well as a strong desire to be with each other.

Combination #3: Both parties have High Passion with at least Average Intimacy and at least Average Commitment

This unusual but not uncommon combination features high energy, satisfying sexual contact, romance, and a willingness to endure adversity, at least by one of the parties. One of you will always wonder what the other party is thinking, but you also know your lover will be there when you need him. Perhaps more importantly, you know you can share your thoughts and feelings without criticism.

The Least Compatible Combinations

Combination #1: Low Passion/Low Intimacy/Low Commitment person with a High Passion/High Intimacy/High Commitment Person

This is the longest shot of all. The basis for a satisfying, fulfilling relationship simply doesn't exist. There will be much tension, stress, confusion, frustration, and emotional withdrawal and a persistent yearning to escape from your partner. Note, however, that during times of adversity (war, famine) many such arrangements are made, and with time and goodwill, an accommodation might be made.

Combination #2: One partner is low in Passion/Commitment and High in Intimacy and the other partner is High in Passion/Commitment and Low in Intimacy

Nothing in this combination suggests a potential for happiness. One partner would dampen the considerable passion of the other, and there would not be enough intimacy and friendship to take the sting out of the constant tension and frustration. You or your lover would always be worried about abandonment, or affairs outside the relationship.

Combination #3: One partner is Low in Passion and Intimacy and High in Commitment and the other partner is High in all three dimensions

Not only would there be sexual frustration and a yearning for caring and friendship on the part of one partner or the other, but worst of all, the high degree of commitment on both sides would prevent or delay the "cure," namely, to say goodbye and (re)search for the correct path.

Combination #4: One partner is Low in Intimacy/Commitment and low in Passion and the other partner is Low in Intimacy/Commitment and High in Passion.

This is a wonderful combination for a couple interested in a torrid love affair and a series of one-night stands. The high sexual energy, the romance, the euphoria during the early phases of the relationship all make this the kind of experience you would want on a cruise ship rather than one to be sanctified on the altar. After the first few months, both will want to bow out of the relationship to search for someone else who fits the exciting-but-aloof-and-unstable bill.

If your compatibility profile falls within the "Most Compatible" category and you have continued to have problems with the relationship, there are other issues, which need to be clarified. Differences in background and values, the motivation for coupling, personality styles and destructive life scripts, and the lack of awareness are among the most probable problem areas. Each of these will be addressed in later chapters. If your compatibility profile falls within the "Least Compatible" category, you now have some idea why you might be having problems.

Ann and Mike completed their Compatibility Scales with the following results:

Ann ranked High on the Passion Scale, the Intimacy Scale and on the Commitment Scale. Her ratings for her "lover" (Mike) suggested that she perceived him to also be High on Passion Scale and on the Commitment Scale but Low on the Intimacy Scale. Interestingly, Mike's ratings for himself were somewhat inconsistent with Ann's: he perceived himself as High in Passion, Average in Intimacy and Average in Commitment. He perceived Ann as high on all three dimensions. The differences suggested mild to moderate difficulty in the relationship unless perceptions changed.

Ann appeared to be the partner who was most willing to give herself to the relationship. On the other hand, she perceived Mike as a highly passionate man who could commit himself to the relationship. This was not totally out of line with Mike's own ratings. The only fly in the proverbial ointment was Ann's perception that Mike's level of intimacy was low. Considering Mike's life script— his father's insistence that logic and intelligence were of greater import than emotional freedom—it wasn't too hard to see why Mike might have had trouble expressing his intimate thoughts and feelings.

At the end of the exercise, Ann asked the unanswered question: "Are we compatible?"

If the profiles were accurate, I told her, it appeared that she and Mike would get along quite nicely under most circumstances. Love-making would be satisfying, and she would never have to worry about Mike's commitment to her or her children. I also noted, however, that she demanded that Mike share inner experiences, and this was very difficult for him. So the answer to Ann's question was, "Yes, you are compatible, but…." I tried to soften the response by observing that the odds favored a good marriage, if that was the route they chose, as long as Mike recognized the problem and prepared himself to work on it. This was not the answer they wanted. They needed more reassurance. Ann and Mike continued their search.

CHAPTER 5
INTIMACY

M ike's relatively low ratings on the Intimacy dimension gave us an opportunity to consider the three dimensions of love in greater detail. In light of the results of the compatibility ratings, I decided to address Intimacy first.

Connecting is the second and in many ways the most difficult phase of coupling. It requires that we appreciate the simplicity of the moment with someone. When we begin to feel we are making love to, rather than with someone, or that we are talking to, rather than with someone, we have already begun a process of exclusion. Intimacy is a process of inclusion, rather than exclusion. The process requires us to make a number of decisions—most of them at an unconscious level—simultaneously.

We must decide, for example, whom we want to participate in our life script. We have our bit players, and our leading women and men. For example, the cashier at the local market is a bit player: she requires little more than a nod in greeting and a "thank you" as we leave the store. Our boss, on the other hand, occupies a position of extreme importance and we might want to—and need to—include him in more of our decision-making than other actors in our life's play.

The person we want most to include in our lives, of course, is our mate or life partner. This is not quite as simple as it sounds: there may be several leading wo/men we wish to consider, and we must then decide which one of these fits the lover-for-life requirements.

After we make that decision, we must then decide how intimate we are willing to be. It would certainly be unusual if we were to tell the cashier, or the cab driver, or the newspaper boy our innermost secrets and desires. They are bit players, and their roles in our lives do not require that they know anything about us other than how they can serve us. Our boss, on the other hand, is someone we may need to include at a deeper level, because our intimate thoughts, desires and fears affect what happens out there in the work world.

Intimacy refers to the degree to which we allow people into our personal lives. Do we dare allow our lover into the deepest layers of our soul where he can see our faults and fears? Or, rather, do we feel more comfortable entertaining him in the foyer of our mind where more general issues are addressed (values, perceptions of the world order, choice of plays, music, etc.)?

The real question is: Can we trust our lover not to abandon us if we allow him to see our wounds from past relationships, or our unattractive habits and attitudes? Shall we allow him to romp freely through our minds and thoughts, letting him comfortably pamper us, argue with us, tease us, criticize us, or give us advice? Or are we more comfortable letting him visit the deepest layers of our personality on the condition that he be quiet and totally accepting?

Time is another factor to be considered. For some of us, intimacy is tolerable only on a time-limited basis: we want our lover to excite our senses and occupy our thoughts—on weekends and holidays. Allowing him into our life at the deepest levels may be OK, but only if we know that the encounter will end in a few days or a few months. Longer periods of closeness may trigger off feelings we don't enjoy, for example, loss of control and boredom.

Ann and Mike were struggling with the process of becoming intimate, of deciding how deeply involved they wanted to become with each other. Ann needed to know what Mike was thinking and feeling, and what his fears and desires were. Mike needed to be more private. He didn't always want to feel that he needed to open up to Ann all the time.

When Ann and Mike entered the second stage of love, the stage where the boundaries between fantasy and reality became blurred, they had begun to examine the role each wants the other to play (bit player, or leading wo / man), how deeply they were willing to let the other person in, and how much freedom they were willing to allow each other to have.

Contact Boundaries

Intimacy requires that we include others in our world. It requires that we share our perceptions and our experiences, our expectations and our beliefs, and, perhaps most importantly, our honesty. Our connection may be smooth or rough. But it must be honest. And with the honesty comes the recognition that both we and our lover exist as sentient beings.

Love is a three-dimensional experience. Intimacy is one of the dimensions: it is, however, an essential dimension. Perhaps a relationship can exist without much passion and without much commitment, but few relationships will succeed without the kind of closeness and attachment that comes with intimacy.

To fully understand what intimacy is all about, we have to understand the concept of "contact boundaries." The contact boundary is the place where we leave off and the rest of the world begins. Everything on this side of my skin is me (mine, our), and everything on that side of my skin belongs to the rest of the world.

When I sit in a chair and feel it pressing against my body, the point where I feel it becomes the contact boundary. There is contact at the skin level of my body. It is the place where I am separated from you (yours, everything which is not me) yet connected to you. If the chair is soft and yielding, the contact is a gentle one. If, on the other hand, it is hard and ungiving, the contact is less comfortable.

The boundary is the point at which we make contact with the outside world: the smell of flowers, the power of the sunset, the hardness of an angry look. It is the place where changes take place. It is the place where I can exchange the things in me for the things I need out there. I can, for example, exchange the carbon dioxide in my lungs for the oxygen in the atmosphere. Or I can exchange the happiness (sadness) in my heart for the warm and tender hug of a friend.

Contact boundaries can be OK, too rigid, or too loose. If the boundary is OK, I know who I am. I know what belongs to me and what belongs inside me (feelings, thoughts, and fantasies). With this knowledge, I can make constructive decisions about the world and my role in it. I know, for example, that my knowledge and my skills are my own, and I won't allow anyone to convince me that my work (thoughts, feelings) belong to them.

The contact boundary, however, can become too rigid. I may have decided at an early age that the world beyond the skin is dangerous. I then create an impermeable membrane between you and me (that is, everything outside my skin boundary). I keep all my feelings and desires inside the thing I have come to know as me; I do not share my laughter or my anger or my sadness, because it is simply too unsafe. My bad early experiences might have taught me that to laugh or become openly angry would leave me vulnerable to criticism and/or abandonment. Nor will I allow your feelings and thoughts to enter my world. You—the world outside my skin—have become an alien world filled with demons I don't understand. My boundaries have become rigid. The result, of course, is the feeling of isolation and exclusion. Many people have survived the unyielding boundary. We regard them as recluses, iconoclasts, and tyrants.

If my boundaries are too loose, I become everything I see, hear, touch, or feel. I (con)fuse with the environment. If a murder is committed in France, I call the police and tell them I did it. If I am a waitress or a nurse, I ask the customer or patient, "What are we having today?" or "How are we doing today?" If I am a schizophrenic, I see myself as part of the world (not confused; simply fused): I am the lamp, the President of the United States, my father or my mother. I may believe my thoughts are being broadcast all over the world. What is inside me filters through a too permeable membrane; my rage, my impulses, my fears, and my desires are uncontrolled and uncontrollable.

Conversely, what is outside of my skin-boundary filters into my body. Your anger angers me; your fear frightens me; your impulses excite me. I have little control over the flow of my energy. My emotions don't know where to go, how to get there, or at what speed. My boundaries are too permeable, and reality becomes hazy. Because I have no clear idea of what is real and what is fantasy, I behave inappropriately.

The contact boundary, then, is like an aura, an energy field. If the field expands, the world (including my lover) outside my skin becomes part of me; if the energy field contracts, the world outside my skin (including my lover) is excluded.

If we are unhappy, pouty, sullen, emotionally withdrawn, or depressed, we recede to a place deep inside us, making it difficult to maintain contact with the outside world and with each other. The greater the upset, the greater the withdrawal. It is often at this point in the relationship we seek couples' counseling or individual psychotherapy. The major complaint, of course, is that there is "no communication;" that is, we no longer trust our partner with our thoughts and feelings; we no longer trust our partner inside us.

When, on the other hand, we are able to expand our contact boundaries at the same time as our partner does, there is a merging of the love-energy fields, and, instead of two separate auras, we find one large one surrounding the two of us. We begin to experience each other in a different way; we experience "intimacy," a closeness born of shared boundaries and shared energies. Our boundaries dissolve. Rather than fearing "intrusion" or "abandonment," we freely enter and freely exit each other's mind, body, and soul. All judgment is suspended. We accept each other uncritically. We feel a deep sense of pride, beauty, and dignity.

Falling in love is an intense but limited sort of intimacy. The sharpness of the experience brings excitement, and the excitement produces an ambiance of trust. The trust is limited, however, because time and experience have not tested it.

Being in love clearly is a different event. We have seen our lover in a variety of situations—when she is angry, or sad, or embarrassed. Despite the discomfort, we continue to accept her uncritically over a relatively long period of time. The difference lies in the level of intimacy, the shared boundaries we enjoy. With intimacy, we not only survive, but we thrive happily!

Being in love is also different from "puppy love." The difference lies, to a large degree, in the depth of intimacy. The thirteen-year-old student who has a crush on her teacher is not involved in a love relationship because (presumably) the teacher's contact boundary has not merged with the student's. Camaraderie and companionship are less intense instances of intimacy in that only specific kinds of boundaries are shared—sports, a cocktail at lunch, or perhaps local gossip.

Intrusion and Abandonment

Imagine that each of us swings on a pendulum. On one side of the pendulum lies the Fear of Intrusion. On the other side of the pendulum is the Fear of Abandonment. The pendulum swings between these two poles of emotional experience. Some of us swing more toward the Intrusion side; others of us, more toward the Abandonment side. Most of us tend to stay somewhere within a broad middle range.

The Intrusion-Abandonment phenomenon is particularly important, because it affects the quality of our intimacy, our passion, and our commitment. When we swing toward the Intrusion side, we become nervous, panicky, or sometimes enraged, because we sense someone is trespassing into our emotional space. We become suspicious and querulous. We begin to show annoyance and irritability.

If we are relatively intact emotionally, we will begin to strengthen the boundaries to keep the intruder out. Sometimes, however, the boundary defenses cannot be reinforced, and we find ourselves feeling paranoid. (The paranoid person is fearful of even minor intrusions, and he can become quite unmanageable when an unwanted visitor knocks at the boundary door).

When we swing toward the Abandonment side, we sense that our lover is "leaving" us. The "abandonment," of course, often is not real. It usually stems from a distortion of an event. A slight criticism or an expression of dissatisfaction is all the ammunition we need to prove that we are not loved anymore. Our behavior then becomes childlike: we cling, we apologize, we manipulate by becoming "ill" or pouty. All of this has only one goal—to keep us from feeling lonely and "abandoned."

Most of us will have a tendency to swing one way or the other; but not many of us can tolerate either too much intrusiveness or too much abandonment. Finding the place where we feel most comfortable is not easy. Some people swing wide and fast until they lose control. Histrionic and Bipolar patients often complain about their uncontrollable swings of emotions, including fear and rage.

The Importance of Attachment and Intimacy

The quality of intimacy we experience as adults reflects the quality of intimacy we experienced as children. And the quality of intimacy we experience as children depends in large part on the quality of our attachment to parents and other caretakers.

If we carefully observe infants directly after birth, we find that even within the first few hours after delivery, the infant, if placed on the mother's stomach, will crawl upward in search of mother's breast. Mother's willingness to first nourish the infant in the womb and then to nourish the infant on demand as it enters the world becomes one of the most important developmental events in a growing child's life. As adults, it also becomes one of the very major ingredients in developing trusting and secure relationships with potential mates and/or lovers.

An infant's experiences with his caretakers during the first few months serve as a model for how the world will treat him in the future, and will influence his expectations of love objects. The process of attaching himself to caretakers takes place unconsciously, but its effects are far reaching. Any disruption in the attachment process alters the infant's perception of his world. The results are entirely predictable. Infants raised in a loving environment feel secure in their love relationships. They develop a positive self-regard, feelings of esteem, compassion, and sensitivity.

On the other hand, infants whose attachment has been damaged for any one of a number of reasons (e.g., abuse, neglect, the lack of adequate parenting, emotional withdrawal of his caretaker, parent's alcohol or drug abuse, emotional illness, or severe loss) develop insecure attachments and learn to view the world as an emotionally cold and hostile place. All dimensions of development are affected: physical, emotional, social, and moral. These early (preverbal) perceptions and accompanying attitudes and behavior persist through adulthood.

Among couples where one partner has an attachment disorder, we find distressing personal interactions, anger, rage, cyclical patterns of depression, poor self-esteem, an absence of feelings of safety and security, a lack of trust, and a high demand for personal attention. Deception, lying, and lack of remorse appear regularly among the complaints of couples seeking counseling.

At times, we find a compulsive self-reliance. The attachment-disordered partner attempts to avoid feelings of closeness by neither needing nor being needed by others. At other times, we find the opposite, compulsive care-seeking, characterized by the urgent and the frequent need for consolation and freedom from personal responsibility. A third common observation suggests angry withdrawal, where one of the partners feels that attachment figures are inaccessible. This is especially true when the partner's demand for attention is ignored—at least in his eyes. Even when the attachment-disordered partner wants to withdraw, the withdrawal has a spiteful, vindictive, and angry quality about it. Clearly, early infant losses affect adult intimacy—the very thing that the distressed partner needs in order to "heal" himself. Is it any wonder that intimacy is a major ingredient in a durable and satisfying relationship?

The importance of intimacy and companionship is revealed, at least in part, by the following statistics:

- Widowed, divorced, and single people have significantly higher death rates than married people for both male and female populations between the ages of fifteen to sixty-four.

- Death rates for victims of cancer are significantly higher for unmarried people. The incidence of heart disease, cerebro-vascular disease, and hypertension is significantly higher for unmarried people than for married people. It appears that heartbreak occurs more frequently among unmarried people than among married people—literally as well as figuratively.

- The number of unmarried men who require institutionalization is 50 times higher than for married men. The ratio for unmarried women is 25:1.

- In the mid-1940s a number of observations were made in foundling homes and orphanages. Orphans receiving regular attention, caressing, and cooing, grew and adapted fairly well. Children deprived of attention because of the high infant-to-caretaker ratio, or who were given only the barest of essentials, soon showed signs of a deep and unrelenting depression, later known as an "anaclitic" depression. They demonstrated little curiosity about, or alertness to, their surroundings. They became "failure to thrive" babies, and once they retreated into themselves, there was little chance they would ever recover. Rene Spitz, the physician attending these children, concluded that without companionship and consistent physical attention, "the spine shrivels" and the child is lost.

- Studies in England at the end of World War II sought to determine the effect of the Blitzkrieg bombing raids on young children. One of the interesting findings was that children who were with their primary caretakers, generally their mothers, at the time of the raids, were able to get over the trauma. However, those children who were by themselves at the time of the bombings were traumatized beyond repair. Years later, even after intensive psychoanalysis, they continued to exhibit fear and anxiety disorders.

- Observations in medical facilities also provide dramatic insight into the power of human companionship. In one study, researchers found that the mere touch of a nurse's hand reduced a patient's heart rate by 30 beats per minute. In another study, two comatose patients responded to the touch of a human hand when no other stimulus could elicit changes in the patient's condition.

The need for emotional and physical closeness is so strong that often the feeling of "intimacy" will be imagined even if there is no valid basis for it. This is especially true early in a relationship. During the contacting and connecting stages, erotic thoughts and sexy feelings are often misperceived and distorted. They are treated like whole realities when they are, in fact, merely reflections of the need for intimacy. Sadly, we often discover, after committing ourselves to a particular notion of what the relationship is all about, we have merged with the wrong person at the wrong time.

When the intimacy is real, however, there is a sense of "we-ness" rather than "I-ness" and there is the relief of loneliness! Is it any wonder that we will do virtually anything to find someone with whom we can create intimacy?

CHAPTER 6
PASSION AND LOVE

The English language is less subtle than many other languages: Spanish, French, and Italian, for example, are more pleasant to the ear and often use fewer words to describe highly complex ideas. Nowhere is this more clear than in our attempts to describe how "romance," "passion," "intimacy," and "love" are the same and yet somehow different. Our popular literature frequently uses these concepts interchangeably. For our purposes, however, defining "passion," one of the three dimensions of what we are calling "love," is essential.

Part of the problem is that there are different fundamental meanings of "love." The ancient Greeks used the word "agape" to refer to love as a godly state of altruism and self-sacrifice; "philia," on the other hand, connoted loyalty and brotherly/sisterly love, while the word "eros" suggested sexual desire and longing.

In Plato's myth of Adrogyne, man and woman were combined as same-sex and opposite-sex couples. Each couple—man/man, man/woman and woman/woman—was joined back to back. There were four arms and four legs but a single head with two faces. The god Zeus, in order to subjugate these sets of beings, split each couple down the middle. Each single person was thus incomplete and in order to achieve oneness, s/he had to search out his/her other half. Eros referred to the ardent desire, the profound longing to be complete once again. Sexual union was one of the ways to do this.

We use Passion in much the same fashion that Plato used the idea of eros: in our model, it refers to the motivation, the striving, the ardent search for a person or activities that will complete us as human beings.

Passion is the act of knocking down the doors of life, of squeezing out the juices of this moment, not just in sexual activity but also in all endeavors. There is passion in the act of eating or talking or in appealing for money to aid starving children.

Passion is the streaming of energy from someplace deep inside us—our souls and the souls of a million ancestors. The passion may come out as a curiosity or wonderment, or an orgasm, or as piece or writing or as preachy morality; but in all cases, it reflects our search for a sense of wholeness, immediacy and urgency.

Passion means to surrender to the life force we were born with, free of inhibition, free of distraction, and free of subdued desire. It is made up of biological energy—the results of our genes—and it is made up of our early experiences.

Voices

The energy driving passion is biological; the direction of our passions is psychological. What concerns us here is the direction of passion. For the purposes of our discussion, I want to define the direction—the path—of passion in terms of "voices."

The "voices" are voices we really hear, voices from our past, and voices from the present. They may be sweet or gruff; reasonable, playful, or hardworking; or they may be frightened or angry. Whatever their tone, these voices represent the wishes, the fears, or the spontaneous oohs, aahs, and gasps of people whose attitudes—and platitudes—we have incorporated into our own thinking and into our everyday demeanor.

The voices may say any or all of the following:

Voice #1: "Do what you want to do, I'll love you anyway." This is the voice of the uncritical, totally accepting parent, the parent voice whose passion lies in protecting, rescuing, pampering, and assuming responsibility for others.

Voice #2: "No matter what you do, I won't love you." This is the voice of the totally unaccepting, critical parent whose passion reveals itself in exerting control, making demands, and intimidating others.

Voice #3: "Let's deal just with objective reality because people are too confusing." Here the passion is expressed in the pursuit of an "objective" world, often made up of numbers, computers, and "correct" decisions. Essentially, the third voice is the part of our personality that integrates the parental part of us with the child part of us.

Voice #4: "I want to play. Won't you please join me?" This is the voice of the socialized, happy-go-lucky, spontaneous child. The passion is seen in curiosity, enchantment, and playful interactions with others.

Voice #5: "I am angry or frightened because (1) you push me around, or (2) you won't give me what I want." This is the voice of discontent, frustration and deprivation often associated with the internalized critical parent voice. The passion reveals itself in a missionary zeal for great causes, or perhaps just fighting, the purpose for which is vague and relatively unimportant.

Voice #6: "I am frightened/sad/lonely/panicky." This is the voice of the infant who cannot cope with current realities. The voice is a small one, often appearing in our dreams and nightmares. It says, "I feel so small, weak, and inadequate that I can't deal with big people or big problems." The passion often comes out as art, literature, or in less fortunate situations, a craving for drugs and alcohol.

The path of our passions often takes the form of an alliance with someone willing to take care of our needs. In extreme cases, the path leads to a yearning for the safety of an institution (jail, mental hospital, or frequent visits to the family physician).

The voices, in all cases, come from old tapes we have stored on the many shelves of our minds. Sometimes the tapes are scratchy, and sometimes they are clear; but they are always with us, guiding us, telling us whether we are doing what they want us to do, in an attempt to bring our behavior in line with society's expectations. In many instances, however, the voices lead us unconsciously to feelings of unhappiness or even to acts of self-destruction.

While passion itself is a rumbling volcano of emotion, the voices of passion are responsible for how we express that emotion. They make up one third of the three-dimensional love described in the first chapter. And they serve as a cornerstone of the contact/connection/coupling process.

Ann and Mike heard many of these voices throughout their courtship. They were both people of passion. Every touch and every kiss, every smile and every word, jolted them into an awareness of the now, the never-ending moment when the world outside would disappear, and intimacy and eroticism began to merge.

Ann told the story of their first meeting. Their contact began as a simple greeting, then became fast and focused. As the evening wore on, they found themselves in a love dance, holding each other close and tight, their hearts—so Ann said in the words of a writer—began beating in slow syncopation. Throughout this long dance, their every move was guided by the voices of passion.

Only we hear the voices of our passion, but others see and experience the behaviors the voices promote. During the beginning phases of a love relationship, the contact and connection phases, the voice is generally that of the playful child.

We want to be lifted and twirled around and around, emotionally and physically; we want to laugh and giggle. We want to become dizzy and lose our balance safely just as we did when we were five or six years old—when we spun ourselves around and around until we became too dizzy to stand erect.

It is *Three Little Pigs* time. We sing and dance and play tunes on our mind-flutes. Who's afraid of the Big Bad Wolf? Or involvement? Or commitment? We build our relationship, many of us, with expediency. We can't bother at this point in the relationship with worrisome thoughts about the strength of the relationship's foundation. We simply want excitement and companionship. Like the songbird in a tree, we whistle and chirp, hoping that our song is heard and returned by the songster on the next branch. The melody is relatively unimportant; the responsiveness and the harmony, however, are important. They signal acceptance and a willingness to play. We are asking, "I want to play...won't you join me?" What we hope to hear is, "Of course I'll play. You sing so well and you're so pretty."

The playful child's voice is not the only voice we hear. We also hear the voice of fear, uncertainty, and at times even panic. Ann tells Mike she is "frightened and confused"; Mike tells Ann he doesn't know what is expected of him. Each is responding to the voice of insecurity and anxiety. It is the voice of their parents' own fears about the real world beyond the skin. It is the voice they hear when they don't know how to act, the voice they hear when they are frustrated, and the voice they hear when they are afraid they will be rejected. At the deepest level, it's the voice we all hear when we are afraid we will mess ourselves and no one will like us anymore—the voice that tells us we should feel shame.

Shame is a key concept here. Shame is a Band-Aid over an imaginary wound. We don't know where the wound is or what it looks like, but we are scared to death that someone will yank that Band-Aid off and reveal the most hideous, the most repulsive something ever created. So we walk around protecting the Band-Aid, making sure no one gets close enough to peek underneath, or even to ask about it. We guard it and we pamper it, all the while feeling repelled by it. If we sense we cannot protect the imagined blemish, we put yet another Band-Aid on top of the first one, and then add more until we are satisfied that no one will ever see what was never there in the first place!

Why are Ann and Mike so frightened and confused? Because somehow, they have been convinced that a layer of gauze, a fictitious flaw, is preferable to being what their voices tell them they should be.

These are fertile grounds for passions to develop. Our desire to protect ourselves—and our desire to avoid dealing with our own discomfort—is converted to a desire to protect and to defend those who also have flaws, or who also are confused and frightened. As a result, we may begin to campaign for assistance for the homeless, become volunteers at the local hospital, or become consumed by the plights of unborn children.

As noted, the path of our passions is dictated by the "voices." If the uncritical parent voice dominates, we are prone to invest our energies in a venture of altruism. The altruism may simply take the form of contributions to a charity or volunteerism. In the extreme, however, it may take the form of self-sacrifice to protect the less fortunate.

If the never-satisfied, demanding, finger-pointing voice of the critical parent dominates, we most likely involve ourselves in more dictatorial pursuits. At one end of the "dictatorial" spectrum, we find the harsh but well-meaning parent who simply wants to raise his child properly; at the other end, we find the mean-spirited bully who subjugates entire nations.

The passion displayed by Mike and Ann is the same kind of passion most of us know quite well. Often the voices say the same kind of things: "Do this" or "Don't do that," or "Let me out of here!" How we negotiate the demands of the voices, however, differs from person to person.

We may make excuses for our behavior and withdraw from the scene. We may recall personal experiences, or the vignettes played out between our parents, and create a voice (uncritical parent) that assures us that all will be OK. Or perhaps we reframe the scene and pull the fangs out of the fearful/hurtful situation, making it less toxic by giving it "more perspective."

If we are truly creative, we figure out a way not only to overcome the obstacle to our happiness, but also to maintain a sense of pride and dignity.

During the beginning phases of our love relationships, the passion we feel is a romantic passion of excitement, giddiness, playfulness, mild insecurity, and a strong desire for physical closeness. As the relationship evolves and matures, all of these feelings are subsumed by other passions: the passion of protectiveness, the passion of acceptance, and the passion partnership.

At one point, according to Ann's story, Mike told her, "Shh, pretty lady, all will be fine." He was telling her that he would not let the Big Bad Wolf break down the door.

At another point, Ann told Mike that she was "more sure than anything" that she wanted him to stay a weekend with her. What Mike heard was the voice of the nurturant (uncritical) parent saying, "I find you acceptable even if you feel embarrassed (weak, small, and ashamed) sometimes."

Rarely do the harsh and demanding critical voices reveal themselves during the initial stages. This would scare off most potential mates. Nor do we expose our "Let's deal with reality" voice too early because—if we are socially aware people—we have learned this voice not only dampens the excitement of the first contact, it does something worse: it bores other people. The seriousness of the voice becomes intrusive and invokes a something less than playful response.

While we rarely reveal the critical voice, or the all-business voice, or the angry voice, it does happen under two general conditions:

- When we sense the other person wants and needs to be criticized, degraded, or belittled, we subconsciously use our critical parent voice to accommodate. If our partner endures the humiliation for anything more than a second, we zero in until we draw emotional blood. These kinds of relationships are common. Early mild criticism leads to later major criticism; early demands lead to later major demands; early rage has the potential for tissue damage in the later stages.

- In the second instance, the critical voice appears when our potential mate reminds us of a particular time, person, or event in our life. For example, if we had an abusive relationship with our parents when we were younger, we might experience "post-traumatic stress," a disorder often characterized by the need to "act out" certain feelings and behaviors that we were too helpless to resist. This phenomenon commonly occurs during wartime when soldiers and noncombatants experience the trauma of battle and the accompanying violence.

If we were abused as children, we will often become abusive as adults. If we have been beaten or frightened as children, or if we have witnessed violence in one form or another, the chances are that we will become an adult at risk for violence. The wrath of the unconscious but fully activated critical (violent) voice we ingested as youngsters is the reaction to seemingly innocent comments of our lover.

A Voice Exercise

To help them better understand the impact of the "voices of passion," I asked Ann and Mike to complete the following exercise:

Remember your (1) first contact, (2) first real date, (3) first time you became intimate (either sexually or emotionally or both). Recall the "voices" you heard from each other. Were they whiny, playful, disappointed, intimidating, pouty, stubborn, sexy, demanding, sweet, frightened?

Ann related her feelings on their first date. "Mike called to ask me out to dinner. It was the first time we had really considered the possibility of dating although we each knew we were attracted to the other. I remember his voice during the telephone call. It was so uncertain, so insecure, that I remember thinking that I wished I could make this easier for him. Even then I wanted to protect him and make him feel ok about the whole situation. The voice I heard was the frightened voice—at least initially—but then, after I said I would love to go out for dinner with him, the voice changed, and he became sort of playful, and we both became giggly.

"I remember feeling like I did when I was in high school and I had a crush on one of the football players, only this time it was a softer, gentler feeling. Not that I didn't feel sexy, but I also felt something deeper. Then one time when I told Mike that my son Jason was ill, he became so attentive—not in a sticky sort of way—just attentive and the voice I heard let me know everything was going to be all right and that I could always count on him. I don't know about the other voices you mentioned. Of course, we've always had passionate discussions about writing and about politics, friendly debates with lots of sparks flying. They're always fun. Other than that, I don't remember any other voices. Wait, maybe when he's really working hard on a project. I hear the voice that seems to need a lot of approval. It's as though he's asking someone to really care about him and what he does. I often wonder what happens if the voice inside his head rejects him and his projects. Maybe that's why he works so hard all the time."

Mike began to tell us about his "voices."

"I remember that first talk we had on the phone. You're right. I was scared. I wanted you to say exactly what you finally did say—that you would be delighted to have dinner with me. I didn't realize my voice came across like a frightened child's. But you're right about that part. The funny thing is that even though I don't remember precisely how I felt, I do remember your voice. You were so gentle, so kind, that whatever fear I had just seemed to melt away. I knew at that point that you were somebody very special. Nobody had ever been able to make me feel that way. And when we went to the restaurant—I think it was in Copley Place—everything was like an adventure. The food we ordered, the bottle of wine, the way you looked at me. The only voice I heard was a romantic and gentle voice. I wanted to skip down the street with you and just hold your hand and touch you.

"Your voices comforted me and made me feel that somehow I fit into your life. It was a strange feeling for me, because I'd been raised to be self-sufficient and I don't let people in too often. You mentioned Jason's illness. What you sensed in me was pretty accurate. I wanted to let you know that I would stand by your side and Jason's side too for as long as it took for him to get better. I didn't realize my feelings came through, but I'm glad you got the message. You are right about another one of my voices. I've never thought about it before, but when I get into one of my projects, I hear two voices. One tells me that I'm really pretty bright and I'm going to win the lawsuit—or whatever the project happens to be. But sometimes I hear a voice telling me that I'm not working hard enough, that I don't deserve to win the case, and no matter how hard I'm willing to work, I'm not acceptable. I don't know whose voice I hear. I think it's a male voice—maybe not—I can't say for sure. I usually end up feeling really tired and I want to sleep or sometimes; when the voice is too strong, I just want to drink myself into a stupor. Since I've met you, I don't hear that voice too often."

"Thank goodness," Ann laughed.

Ann and Mike picked up a variety of messages from each other—largely at an unconscious level. The messages were distilled from the words, the inflection, the intensity, and the benevolence of the "voices" that each one had introjected (swallowed) as a child. Some of the voices were digested and were experienced as belonging to each person's personality. Some of the voices, however, could never be fully digested because they were foreign to the way the person wanted to present himself. The "frightened voice" that Mike experienced was uncomfortable for him because it simply didn't fit into the image he had developed over the years of who he was. Likewise, the "needy" voice he experienced was the antithesis of what he was raised to believe he was, that is, totally self-sufficient. Yet these voices influenced every behavior and every decision that Mike made. Ann was able to subdue the power of the needy feelings by giving Mike unspoken permission to feel helpless and needy. She also responded to his sexiness and his playfulness, feelings that were encouraged by neither Mike's intellectualized father nor his business-like ex-wife.

Ann's voices also influenced her decision-making. Her Playful Child enjoyed being taken out for dinner. Ann could be sexy and playful. At the same time, given Mike's nervousness about possible rejection, she could help alleviate his apprehension by using a protective and gentle voice she learned from her mother and reinforced by her father. She said she really loved the opportunity to nurture him, maybe even mother him a little, while at the same time she could feel the excitement of the physical and emotional closeness that she felt.

Clearly, passion is an essential ingredient in most relationships. But passion is not simply the desire to be romantic; it is a desire to strike a harmonic balance. It is a path that has been formed by many influences. It is a biological life force flowing out through a thousand voices we have swallowed—voices we now use to attract our potential mate and to repel our potential enemies. The trick is to match the correct voice—the correct passion—with the correct recipient in a balanced fashion. Too much of the uncritical parent leads to an unrealistic degree of playfulness; too much of the critical parent leads to rage and/or withdrawal. How much is too much is a decision each person must make in her own way. However, a decision must be made; a relationship without balanced passions is simply one of life's good meals without the spices to make it a great one.

CHAPTER 7
COMMITMENT

One day, as we explored the recipe for a loving relationship, Ann and Mike spontaneously brought up the notion of commitment, what it really means, and why men seem to have so much trouble with the idea that ideally marriage is "for keeps." Ann observed that once when she and Mike attended the wedding of a dear friend, Mike seemed to get "squirmy" when the pastor used the words "til death do you part". In his defense, Mike noted that his squirminess had nothing whatever to do with the words *per se*, that he was reacting to the fact that the couple had already split up a half-dozen times and that he doubted that death would be the only requisite for another break-up. Mike insisted that commitment was not difficult for him, but that finding a woman to commit himself to always had been. As Mike said this, he squeezed Ann's hand gently, and she seemed to understand that commitment might not be as much of a problem as she had once thought it might be.

Common lore holds that women are always ready to commit, but men need a bit of coaxing. Things have changed considerably in this regard. Women have become more independent and self-sufficient. Articles in popular women's magazines counsel readers about the new equality between men and women. They make cogent arguments for women's liberation. The notion of commitment has evolved from the full-time-wife-stay-at-home-with-the-kids caricature into a free-wheeling, self-determined, empowered I-have-a-right-to-be-happy caricature of womanhood. The problem with both of these stereotypes is that neither is real. Reality dictates that each of us negotiates the terms of our intimate relationships. And nowhere is this truer than in the degree and quality of our commitment to our lovers. Before looking at what the process of commitment is all about, let's look at the reasons why people commit.

Men and women are willing to stay together for extended periods of time for three primary reasons: (1) companionship (2) "love" and (3) sexual fulfillment. What most of us want is a relationship based on friendship, mutual trust, mutual respect, and satisfying physical contact. Wo/men who have established a relationship based on these qualities have a better than even chance of making it to the altar (if that is the route they choose). Qualities that increase the odds include the ability to laugh, emotional balance, and a pleasing appearance.

Neither the expanded boundaries of Intimacy nor the sharp urgency of Passion accurately describe the third dimension of love—Commitment. Commitment in its most primitive form is being *there*; and, in its most refined aspect, it is *being* there. At first glance, the difference may be difficult to perceive; but there is a difference, and it is an important one.

Being there means that we "hang around": We are available to our lover just as the oxygen in the air is available to us when we need to revitalize our bodies. When this "being there" experience is coupled with passion and intimacy, our relationships are exciting and nourishing. And they are exciting and nourishing over a long period of time.

However, when the commitment is based on simple convenience, there is neither passion nor intimacy. Being together is all that is necessary to satisfy the requirements of a "committed" relationship.

Changing the emphasis from "being *there*" to "*being* there," with all its subtlety, makes for an entirely different experience for two people. We not only "hang around," we "hang around" in a particular way. We are devoted; we sit on the edge of our lover's boundary always ready to step inside when invited, and ready to withdraw when asked to do so. It is this devotion, this fidelity with a flexible attachment that differentiates the primitive, routine spending-time-together from the energizing and joyful event of being there intimately and passionately.

In an I/Thou relationship, the total commitment is greater than two people resonating within each other's life space. There is no better example of this kind of Commitment than in this (edited) passage from *Sonnets from fhe Portuguese* by Elizabeth Barrett Browning:

When our two souls stand up erect and strong,
Face to Face, silent, drawing nigh and nigher,
Until the lengthening wings break into fire
At either curved point — what bitter wrong
Can the earth do to us, that we should not long
Be here contented? Think!

With Intimacy, we have two people who act as one; with Commitment, we have two people who behave differently. The boundaries are not always shared, but the exchanges at the boundary level are consistent and lend an air of safety and predictability. It is not enough to simply fight life's battles and play "ain't-it-awful-about..." in front of the T.V. Commitment, born of passion and intimacy, implies the desire to fight life's battles together—as a cosmic entity.

When commitment is lacking, we feel we ourselves are lacking. Walls and barriers to happiness spring up unannounced. Here are some of the things we sense intuitively:

- We don't communicate. We don't even attempt to solve problems together. The songster in the other tree responds to our song, but its song is empty of feeling and energy.

- We are mistrustful. The High Commitment person is guarded and vigilant, imagining (often with just reason!) that the sharing of feelings is limited by time. The Low Commitment person also is guarded because he doesn't want to leave the "wrong" impression—the impression he is going to be there for the duration. (Of course, the High Commitment person is aware of this within the first half-hour of the relationship, but is willing to play a long-shot under the guise of patience.)

- We feel insecure and fear rejection. We don't know when "the other shoe will drop" but we are certain it will, and we keep looking for the signs.

- We feel the need for approval from the other person. Whether we are the High Commitment type or the Low Commitment type, we become cautious. We do not want to offend the other's sensibilities. We choose our words cautiously, we behave cautiously, and we think cautiously.

- We lose our flexibility (flex-ability), and we begin to act in a ritualized, highly predictable, cybernetic fashion. We follow one set of beliefs; it can be either our own or our partner's, but in either case the beliefs become rigid and inflexible. Our behavior is designed for one thing: to avoid conflict and, unconsciously, to maintain the status quo. Problems continue to occur without solutions; and, ironically, solutions occur without consciously perceived problems.

- We strive for power and "I'm right-ness." Giving up even a tiny bit of emotional territory is tantamount to an admission of weakness and ineffectiveness. The High-Commitment type wants to prove she is correct to want fidelity and devotion; the Low-Commitment type holds out for higher levels of dedication and loyalty. Neither truly understands that what the other wants is impossible.

- Ultimately, we experience a subdued but pervasive hostility that even high degrees of passion and high degrees of intimacy can't erase. It comes out in the simplest transactions: what to buy, how much to spend at a restaurant, what kind of music is most civilized, whether the Republicans (Democrats) can ever truly represent the will of the people, etc.

Those of us who have observed that this same kind of behavior follows a breakdown in the realms of Passion and Intimacy are, of course, correct. That is why a ripened love is three-dimensional. Each dimension can be independent of the other two, but in mature relationships, the three become the holy trinity of contentment.

In one of the most common compatibility profiles, a High Intimacy-High Passion couple meets and dates for a month or two until it is discovered that one of the two members of the couple is high on the Commitment dimension and the other is low on the Commitment dimension. If there is enough intimacy and passion, the gap between the two levels of commitment may be bridged by time and experience. Generally, however, this is not the case. Rather, the relationship begins to crumble slowly and resentment supplants affection.

Conversely, a relationship characterized by a high level of Commitment and low levels of Passion and Intimacy produces the kind of predictability, stability and sameness generally reserved for inmates serving long prison sentences.

I asked Ann and Mike to fill out the following scale:

Commitment Scale

"Here are ten statements. To the left of each statement write the number that best describes how you feel or behave. Rate each statement according to the following scale":

> 5= Strongly Disagree
> 4=Disagree Somewhat
> 3=Neither Agree nor Disagree
> 2=Agree Somewhat
> 1=Strongly Agree

Rating   Item
_____   1) We don't communicate as much as we did before.
_____   2) We're grouchy and querulous.

_____ 3) My lover is not as available as much as I need for him to be.

_____ 4) I have to compete for time and attention from my lover.

_____ 5) I know it's silly, but I feel shackled to my lover.

_____ 6) I feel too clingy and "needy."

_____ 7) I talk to outsiders about my problems more than I talk to my lover about them.

_____ 8) I find that I worry a lot about what life will be like with my partner twenty years from now.

_____ 9) I find that I seem to need my lover's approval too much.

_____ 10)I feel more insecure now than I did earlier in the relationship.

The lowest score you can receive on this brief test is 10; the highest score is 50. A score in the high range 40-50) suggests that you are in a relationship with someone whom you trust, and who you feel is committed to the relationship.

If Intimacy and Passion are high, a moderate score (20-39) suggests that the relationship may be a comfortable one. Or it may signal that the relationship is changing. Whether the change is positive or negative may be unclear. If insecurity and the querulousness are frequently incurred, it does not bode well for the future. If the scores in these areas are low, however, and the reason for the moderately low scores has to do with the feeling of neediness and approval, time may well provide the healing elements necessary for more commitment and less tension.

Low scores (10 to 19) across the board imply the relationship is being held together by other attributes such as Passion, or perhaps some of the more pragmatic reasons for coupling (see next chapter). This may work out for a while, but when things get tough, the brittleness of the relationship will reveal itself. Of course, there are instances when two High-Passion, High-Intimacy, Low-Commitment people get together with the explicit understanding that the relationship probably won't last forever. It is the exception rather than the rule, but for some people it works out just fine.

In Ann's case, there was no score lower than a "3," suggesting that she wasn't experiencing any seriously disturbing feelings about her relationship with Mike. She did admit to early feelings of neediness, but as they became more comfortable as a couple, Ann became more secure and the clingy feelings subsided.

Mike's ratings on the Commitment Scale were generally lower than Ann's scores. The only low score that really seemed to matter to Ann, however, was on item #8: "I find I worry a lot about what life will be like twenty years from now."

We spent the better part of a session discussing Mike's perception of a "committed" life. There were clear differences between the two people, Ann expressing complete confidence in a happy future and Mike expressing doubts about addressing the future when they couldn't even make decisions about the present! His responses to the other items fell within the average to high average range: He enjoyed his time with Ann, wanted to spend more time with her, and felt that she was willing to accommodate his need for attention. At times he too was bothered by feelings of dependency, but these were manageable. There were no indications of grouchiness or lack of trust. In short, if Ann could tame Mike's apprehension about the future, it would be smooth sailing. The question was: could she do it?

The exploration of the three dimensions of love serves as a backdrop to the following chapters. Often other variables will determine whether the Mikes and the Anns of the world will finally be able to produce a viable togetherness out of an early passionate encounter. Ultimately, they would need to decide whether to terminate the relationship, limit it, maintain it, or expand it.

CHAPTER 8
REASONS FOR COUPLING

I f you ask ten of your dearest single friends why they want to get married, you can anticipate ten different answers, but the chances are that most of the answers will involve the notion of "love." Love, however, is a relatively new phenomenon as far as coupling is concerned.

The history of marriage reveals that before the 1900s, people paired off for a host of reasons having little to do with "love." For example, until the 1970s, dictionaries in the People's Republic of China defined "love" as "a decadent bourgeois silliness." The same kind of sentiment was evident centuries before in Sparta, where unmarried people were often forced into a darkened room. Each picked a partner, unseen and unknown. The goal of Sparta's military rulers was to increase the population, and subsequently to increase the size of the Spartan army. Love played no role in the process. Any man or woman not contributing to the goal bore the full weight of public disdain.

Similarly, Peruvian Incas set one day aside each year for the expressed purpose of arbitrarily assigning each maiden of the village to a bachelor. The experience was not in the least romantic, but it did serve the purpose, which was to increase the population. The European version of this arrangement in feudal times called upon matchmaking and pre-arranged marriages. Practicality was the primary consideration; political alliances, financial mergers, acquisition of land and assets, and pacifying potential enemies were far more important than romantic notions of love.

The results of early "scientific" and psychoanalytic studies of the phenomenon suggest that coupling can reflect any of the following: the universal fear of loneliness, chemical attraction, electricity, magnetism, unconscious mate prototypes, toxic and diseased brains, odors that attract perspective mates, archetypal genes in the male, and geographic proximity. Notably absent from each of these processes is the free-will version of love, which presumably dominates the contemporary coupling experiences of mature adults—at least in the industrial nations.

When we couple with another human being, the event is defined on one side by a commonly unspoken agreement about the exclusiveness of the relationship, and, on the other side, by a wedding celebration, cohabitation, or some other public declaration about our commitment. At this point, we demonstrate the exclusivity of our relationship through "couple" behaviors. In short, we agree to abide by the social rules and norms governing coupled relationships.

Coupling, at any level, is a response to our mutual needs and desires: physical attraction, availability, vitality, energy level, ability to communicate verbally and nonverbally, style of life, intelligence, humor, wisdom, affection and warmth, sexual attraction, personal values, passion, intimacy, and the capacity for commitment. The specific ingredients making up the needs-and-desires smorgasbord vary according to the emotional/social/financial profiles of each person in the relationship. These profiles are made up of wishes and fears that are unique to us and generally not duplicated by others.

With time and experience, each couple develops a unique character that is qualitatively different from the individual traits of singleness contributed by either partner. The amalgamation marks a change in the very nature of the relationship.

One plus one equals more than two when we are involved with others. The admixture of our joint talents, desires, needs, and values is viewed by us and by the outside world as something basically different from what we would exhibit as separate individuals.

Two "weak" characters can produce a "strong" bonding and an enduring relationship. On the other hand, we often find that two "strong" characters can produce a flawed and tenuous coupling.

Some relationships simply are more successful than others. When we examine the elements of successful marriages, we often find the following:

1) The ability of each partner to stand alone if necessary: While each person supports the other in the relationship, neither person is totally dependent on the other. Totally dependent people become "enmeshed" in their relationships. The boundaries become "loose" and ill-defined. One person becomes the other; they see the world through the same eyes. Perceptions of reality become blurred and idiosyncratic. Rather than roaming freely in each other's life space, each unwittingly becomes trapped behind her lover's boundary and cannot find her way out. We speak of this as "confluence"—the merging with our environment. Separate identities no longer exist: Everybody becomes a "we," an unhealthy situation to be sure—especially when the "we" includes at least one partner who is addictive or abusive. This is the atmosphere that produces a co-dependency and, in the worst-case study, co-paranoia, *a folie à deux*, where both parties become partners in the worst crime there is—the destruction of the identity of self.

2) The ability of each person to benefit from the union: Each person's life is socially and emotionally more enriched and more self-actualized than it would be if the other half of the couple didn't exist. The high divorce rate gives testimony to the fact that marriages often fail this simple test of viability: At least one of the partners feels that he isn't fully ripening or benefiting from the relationship. There may be other benefits—security, acceptance by peers and parents, etc., but the essence of life—excitement and growth—is missing.

3) The "Resonance Factor": Each person in a relationship "resonates" at a certain energy level. Like violin strings, two people "vibrating," each one at a slightly different energy level, influences the other and combines with him so that a synergy is developed. The synergy results in an emotional, sexual, and intellectual harmony that produces a lusher, stronger, and more beautiful "chord." The

violinist properly playing two strings at the same time produces a sound that is superior to either string played singly. In the same sense, two "weak" partners can often be part of a synergistic relationship that results in a strength and harmony.

These three qualities produce stability, symmetry, and stamina in the relationship—qualities that often elude individuals on their own. They also enable couples to smooth out emotional hills and valleys— the occasional imbalances that every relationship must endure.

Whether we like to admit it or not, each of us carries a shopping list of ingredients while searching for our soul mate. Some ingredients are fairly obvious: geographical compatibility, similarity of background and values, physical attraction (height, weight and "prettiness"), age, religion, occupation, intelligence, creativity, and lifestyle.

For the romantic couple, there really is only one path to follow when deciding whom to choose as a mate. As Carlos Castaneda suggested:

"Look at every path closely and deliberately, then ask yourself a crucial question: 'Does this path have a heart?' If it does, the path is good; if it doesn't, it is of no use."

In reality, however, there are sometimes not-so-readily admitted reasons why we choose to become part of someone's life: immigrants desiring citizenship, a parent who wants a mother/father for the children, young wo/men who want someone to take care of them, money and wealth, social status...the list goes on.

Motivation played a vital role in Ann's relationship with Mike. They were happy with each other but they were worried that their motivations for becoming a couple were different. Ann wanted someone who could share her love of literature, someone who could show passion, and mostly, she said, she wanted someone who would stand by her side no matter what. For his part, Mike wanted a woman who could analyze life events dispassionately when necessary. He also enjoyed passion and the sense of commitment, he said, but there were other reasons why people get together.

By the end of the session, it was clear that the couple really did show some differences in what they wanted—what drove them to seek out a mate for life. They were discouraged. Could they possibly overcome their differences, they wanted to know. Were their motives for getting into a relationship so different that it just couldn't work out for them? It was time for a more objective approach to the issues surrounding the motivation for coupling. I gave each one a scale entitled simply, Reasons for Coupling and asked them to bring back the completed forms the following week. Below is the scale in its entirety:

Motivations for Coupling Scale

Below are fifty reasons why people become involved. Rate each reason along a three-point scale. The objective is to determine whether the reason is "Very Important," "Somewhat Important," or "Not Important." Simply circle the number next to the phrase that best describes your motivation for becoming involved with your partner. To be fully effective, both parties should complete the scale.

Degree of Motivation

	Low	Average	High
1. Intimacy	1	2	3
2. Sexual Attraction	1	2	3
3. Pity	1	2	3
4. Fear	1	2	3
5. Hero Worship	1	2	3
6. Mutual Interest	1	2	3
7. Feeling Needed	1	2	3
8. Feel Indebted	1	2	3
9. Admiration	1	2	3
10. Prearranged Marriage	1	2	3
11. Natural Thing To Do	1	2	3
12. Afraid to Hurt Partner	1	2	3
13. Desire for Family	1	2	3

	Low	Average	High
14. Professional Growth	1	2	3
15. Financial Security	1	2	3
16. To Stop Working	1	2	3
17. Property	1	2	3
18. Reduce Taxes	1	2	3
19. Social Pressure	1	2	3
20. Leave Parents	1	2	3
21. Rebel / Parents	1	2	3
22. To Please Parents	1	2	3
23. Improve Social Life	1	2	3
24. Pregnancy	1	2	3
25. For Spite	1	2	3
26. Blackmail	1	2	3
27. Parent for Children	1	2	3
28. Prove I'm Not Gay	1	2	3
29. U.S. Citizenship	1	2	3
30. Legalize Cohabitation	1	2	3
31. Care for Me	1	2	3
32. Care for Parents	1	2	3
33. Loneliness	1	2	3
34. To Share Problems With	1	2	3
35. To Prove I am Desirable	1	2	3
36. Biological Clock	1	2	3
37. Want to Settle Down	1	2	3
38. Boredom	1	2	3
39. On the "Rebound"	1	2	3
40. Spiritual Development	1	2	3
41. Need a Housekeeper	1	2	3
42. Punish Myself	1	2	3
43. To Experiment with Life	1	2	3
44. To Keep Me Young	1	2	3
45. To Rebuild My Life	1	2	3

	Low	Average	High
46. Sense of Humor	1	2	3
47. Friendship	1	2	3
48. To Fend Off Enemies	1	2	3
49. Passion	1	2	3
50. Commitment	1	2	3

After completing your ratings, answer the following questions:

Does your lover really satisfy the motivation for your wanting a relationship?

Yes _____   No_____

If not, in what ways doesn't s/he?

If through this exercise you have discovered that your reasons for coupling with your partner are not the same reasons for his/her coupling with you, consider the consequences. Why have both of you continued a relationship that may not work? What keeps you from terminating it?

Review your answers to these questions. Based on what you have said about the reasons for getting together with partner, circle the number on the scale below which indicates the "risk of failure":

Compatible		Incompatible
1 2 3	4 5 6 7	8 9 10
Minor Risk	Average Risk	High Risk

When we next met, Ann told me that she and Mike had agreed on a dozen reasons for being together. Passion, Intimacy, Friendship, and Sexual Attraction were Very Important and each believed the other party felt the same way. For Ann, having mutual interests, feeling needed, financial security, having someone care for her, and having a father for her two sons were also Very Important. Mike and Ann rated Humor high on the list of motivations. The one area that seemed to bother them was "Commitment." Ann scored her commitment as Very Important and perceived that it was not nearly as important for Mike.

For his part, Mike rated Commitment "Important" for both of them, noting that Ann had often said that she didn't need marriage or a diamond ring to legitimatize the relationship. This difference in their ratings led to a discussion about "mixed messages" and honest communication. When asked to answer the questions at the end of the rating scale, neither had trouble: both agreed that their ability to be intimate at every level was the crucial ingredient in the relationship, and they agreed that the risk of their relationship failing was minor.

What became clear from our discussions about the motivation for getting together and staying together was how differently each person saw himself. Ann and Mike each had a different "slant" on life. For Ann, romance and passion mixed with security and humor were the most important considerations. For Mike, finding someone with whom he felt secure enough to be intimate was most important. He also liked the idea that he had discovered a partner who would be open to new experiences. He had been on a quest for spiritual growth for years and enjoyed studying the Eastern religions. Ann shared his enthusiasm for visiting the Orient and becoming acquainted with Buddhism and Taoism.

We learned that Ann and Mike had each found a source of personal completion from someone who could satisfy his external needs. The question now was whether each was emotionally comfortable with the other.

CHAPTER 9
TROUBLE IN PARADISE

While our ability to suppress feelings allows us to adapt to a "chilly" emotional climate in our relationships, unconsciously (and sometimes not so unconsciously) we continue to experience a nagging doubt—a quiet irritation—that no amount of "adjusting" will relieve. The result is that we often find ourselves in uncomfortable and destructive relationships.

The emotional climate of a relationship refers to the degree to which we feel comfortable with our lover—the degree to which we can tolerate the "flat" notes of the relationship. Emotional climates can be extreme: relationships can be too "cold" or too "hot." But, then again, people differ in their ability to tolerate extremes. Eskimos adapt nicely to extreme cold; the natives of the Amazon rainforests learn to tolerate extreme heat.

Just as weather consists of wind, rain, and low and high-pressure systems, the emotional climate of our relationships consists of a flow of behavioral pressures between our lover and us. Many of the behaviors are too subtle to define in everyday terms. They are made up of changes in mood, faint changes in body posture and facial gestures, and changes in energy levels. There is no real vocabulary to describe these changes, but we can feel them, just as we can sense the flat note in an aria. Too many disturbing emotional reactions make the climate inhospitable and uncomfortable. On the other hand, even the harshest emotional climates can offer varying degrees of emotional comfort depending on our emotional needs.

Whether they could tolerate the overall climate of their relationship—and its occasional inclement weather—was the question Ann and Mike dealt with here. The goal was to help them appreciate their emotional "comfort zones."

Our discussion of emotional climates began with an overview of basic personality types and ended with a method to measure emotional climates. To help Ann and Mike understand what I meant by "inhospitable" emotional climates, I identified and described a variety of personality styles, all of which taken to the extreme can become "toxic" to a love relationship. After listening to the descriptions, Ann noted with a smile, "But we're all like that!" And indeed we are, but most of us —at least most of the time—don't make other people feel crazy.

Crazy-makers are people who drive us crazy. Their behavior, their suspicions, and the way they think make us feel edgy and frustrated. They possess certain traits that most of us find difficult to accept and even more difficult to deal with. The first four major toxic personalities are described in detail. These descriptions are followed by vignettes of other potential lovers who are hard to cozy up to because of their coldness, clinginess, or lack of authenticity. Most are easy to spot on a first date if you know what to look for and how to look for it.

The Obsessive Thinker

The Obsessive Thinker is robotic, highly efficient, regimented, detail-oriented, deliberate, and persistent. Unfortunately, he is also rigid in his thinking, driven in his behavior, and confused about what is socially acceptable. He sets himself apart from others because of his strong opinions, and his narrow definitions about what is right and what is wrong. There are no gray areas in his life. He is oppositional and negative—at least superficially. When we listen closely, however, we find something even more annoying. We find that we become frustrated, not because of any real negative contact, but because there is no real contact at all. We get the feeling we are talking into a cobweb. Except for an occasional attentive gaze, there is no indication that he hears our words, or that he has understood our message. If we offer an observation or an opinion, the Obsessive Thinker generally responds with a "yes… but." The maddening part of the exchange is the never-satisfied tone of his responses; it is as though he asks us for our thoughts, but won't acknowledge them once they are given.

At a deeper level, the Obsessive Thinker's problem is his inability to pay attention. He misses the whole point of the conversation. He simply can't shift gears and come up with a different way of looking at things. He is distracted by a particular point of view and rigidly adheres to it—not necessarily in a nasty or hostile manner, although his irritability is clear.

The whole of his existence, intellectual and emotional, lies in the details of any given situation. He exudes intensity and a narrowing of focus that excludes the larger picture of life. Casualness and spontaneity are subjugated to a microscopic regard for non-essentials. The tiniest scratch on a recording becomes more important than the melody of the song.

The Obsessive Thinker generally is productive. In fact, he produces all the time. Long hours, hard work, and intense concern about his level of achievement impress supervisor and workmates alike. Nonetheless, rather than stir up feelings of admiration, his successes are regarded as an oddity or, even worse, not regarded at all. His attention to detail consumes him. He sees his goals clearly and strives toward perfection. As a worker, he involves himself in minutiae, often choosing jobs that require technical skill rather than "people skills."

What makes him so unique is the almost constant need to put forth effort, a need that taxes the patience of co-workers and lovers alike. The Obsessive Thinker is always trying—trying to succeed, trying to do better, and trying to maintain a semblance of order in his life through activity. That his inner voices exclude playfulness is a trait that makes him a poor candidate for the casual date.

If you listen to the Obsessive Thinker for even a few minutes, you will hear many references to what people "should" or "ought to" do. His speech is riddled with finger-pointing words—words that bring guilt and shame. But, again, he doesn't really mean it; he just can't help it. The pressure he exerts on others, and the anxieties he experiences *ad nauseum* are the result of the many "shoulds" he swallowed early in life. His wishes, whimsical thoughts, spontaneity, and anything else that distracts him from his work or from putting order in his life produces restlessness and tension. Under the pressure of this anxiety, the tiny cracks in his personality widen, and, instead of a highly efficient and productive man, we see a taskmaster grappling with the possibility of losing control.

A key concept here is "role." For the Obsessive Thinker, a "role" is the schematic of the shoulds and have-to's of his life. We can imagine him saying to himself, "I am (my role is) a lover, therefore I should do such and such…" or "I am an engineer, therefore I have to do such and such.…"

The role serves as a skeletal outline he fills in with appropriate expectations and procedures. He colors in the shoulds of his life with what he regards as acceptable behavior. Any deviation is punished by the all-pervasive anxieties and worries that he is doing something wrong—a taboo in the Obsessive Thinker's religion of orderliness and moral necessity. We realize before the end of the first date that his driven behavior and rigid boundaries banish us from the inner chambers of his soul.

Ironically, the Obsessive Thinker's steadfast reliance on making correct decisions about what is acceptable belies his near helplessness in decision-making. Because he is so concerned with the rightness of his decisions, he tries to balance the pluses and the minuses of any decision—over and over, and over again. He constantly worries and struggles. He constantly weighs consequences (butchers and Obsessive Thinkers weigh everything!). He becomes obsessed with right answers and correct behaviors until he is exhausted—and until he exhausts us.

Imagine the agony of the Obsessive Thinker when asked what color suit he likes or what kind of wallpaper he would like in his living room. The problem again in a situation like this is the absence of a rule that limits choices—the absence of a should that automatically dictates a right answer.

The Suspicious Thinker

Suspicious Thinkers also pay attention to details. But they are interested in a different kind of detail. Obsessive thinkers pay attention to minutiae—the details of details. The essentials of life seem to escape their scrutiny. The Suspicious Thinker, on the other hand, is focused on subtle behaviors—glances, words, suggestions, and facial expressions—that he suspects are designed to trick him. He becomes apprehensive, anxious, and preoccupied with the thought that someone is out to get him. No amount of talking, arguing, or logic can convince him otherwise.

When the Suspicious Thinker's distrust is chronic, the resulting emotional climate is tense and extremely uncomfortable. The level of discomfort affects all three dimensions of love: passion, intimacy and commitment. His relationships suffer because of his keen perception and his often brilliant insight, as much as from his suspicious scrutiny. In short, he won't let people get away with a thing. He seems to see everything, and to know everything. At least he sees whatever he needs to see in order to confirm his suspicions.

He searches endlessly. He tells us he wants to get to the "bottom line," the "essence" of the relationship. He says he wants to deflate pretense and sham, and to enter into an "honest" relationship. But what he really wants is a careful analysis of events, from which is excluded any information that contradicts his suspicions.

What sets the Suspicious Thinker apart from most people is his habitual and active search patterns. The same level of inspection he reserves for lovers is applied to all experiences. He scrutinizes pictures, documents, agreements, and math problems with gusto. He is hyper-alert and sensitive to anything out of the ordinary. He tells us he is searching for truth, but we wonder whether his real motivation is to find the truth before the truth finds him. The climate of his relationships reflects confusion and unpredictability—emotions that do not enhance fun, humor, a casual date, a good-morning breakfast, or an honest disagreement.

In part, the Suspicious Thinker is motivated by the need to know precisely what is going on in the relationship. When we look carefully at his actions, however, we see that he is interested in something more, namely, in discovering his "truth" at the cost of our credibility. His self-righteousness, his finger-pointer attitudes, his intrusiveness, and his insistence on "honesty" dampen a night on the town at any cost. He resists our attempts to confront him with logic; temper outbursts, and, of course, suspiciousness, follow any attempt on our part to inject reason into a debate of issues.

Everyday experiences that most of us take for granted become "clues" to the Suspicious Thinker. The facts he sees are the very same facts we see, but their significance is interpreted differently. He draws connections between experiences that most of us wouldn't. Most of us would agree, for example, that taxes are necessary; the Suspicious Thinker, however, carries the idea further. He may believe it is part of a government plot to rob us of our money, to subjugate us, and to "keep the little guy in his place." Though socialism is generally seen as an economic and social philosophy, the Suspicious Thinker might see it as part of a global political takeover. (Of course, the suspicious Socialist sees Capitalism in the same light.) While the Obsessive Thinker sees the details of details and yearns for perfectionism, the Suspicious Thinker searches for imperfections that become the clues to imagined schemes and manipulations.

Suspicious Thinkers involved in a relationship become possessive and jealous. A lover observed to receive an innocent kiss from a family friend becomes a partner in an affair. The boss who shows up late for an appointment becomes part of the plot to force the Suspicious Thinker's resignation. The slightest rejection—a grimace or smile at the wrong time, a subtle attempt at correction—meets with a look of tension, close investigation, and perhaps even rage.

Most of us, if we are even modestly normal, are able to shrug off rejection. We use our social skills to push them aside, or we simply repress the incident and get on with our lives. Very often we are able to use humor to defuse our annoyance, or to mollify our anxious concerns. Not so with the Suspicious Thinker, who is more likely to become enraged and vindictive. At this point in a relationship, the tension becomes so draining and so uncomfortable that the habitually Suspicious Thinker becomes a person we most want to avoid. Fortunately, while all Suspicious Thinkers distort reality to some degree, and while most can drive us crazy with their suspicions and jealousy, most do respond to love and caring.

The Non-Thinker

The Non-Thinker is quite different from the Obsessive Thinker and the Suspicious Thinker. He does not see the details of the details, nor does he search for clues of a "plot" or "trickery." He sees the world as a bunch of unconnected dots onto which he projects his fears and wishes. He is an impressionist. He is not interested in facts or objective data. Introduced to a stranger, he may gush, "S/he's great," "Wonderful," or "Unbelievable," or perhaps, "S/he's awful," "Disgusting," or "Nerdy," without any information whatsoever upon which to base his conclusions.

The Non-Thinker senses and intuits the world. Colors are readily transmuted to shapes and sounds. The sight of a full moon or perhaps the music of Vivaldi readily induce an altered state of consciousness; the bizarre juxtapositions of a Picasso painting induce feelings of sadness or anger as much as they inspire awe. Paris isn't simply Paris: it is a bouquet of flowers in a field of weeds. Asked to explain his perceptions, he responds, "It just looks that way—I don't know why."

Unlike the Obsessive Thinker or the Suspicious Thinker, the Non-Thinker depends on immediate sensations and hunches. He lacks the persistence and narrowed focus we see in the other kinds of crazy makers. He is neither overdriven, terribly efficient, nor intellectually curious, although he is often capable of creative problem solving. He becomes easily distracted, goes off on tangents, and his thinking is hard to follow. Unusual ideas grab his attention; he is susceptible to compelling outside influences. We get the impression that he is dragged from pillar to post by anything he finds stimulating—emotions, words, colors, or sounds.

Emotionally, he is given to quick changes. He can be easily embarrassed, overwhelmed with grief, full of apologies, become silly and giddy, and exhibit tantrums—all within a brief few moments. He flits from one stimulus to another and from one subject to another without the benefit of control or good judgment. Bad feelings and good feelings become fused into one global undifferentiated response to his immediate surroundings. The most unique characteristic of the Non-Thinker is his shallow existence.

Emotions flow abundantly, but we're left with the impression that the Non-Thinker doesn't really feel them at all. He reminds us of a character in a cartoon. His emotions are interchangeable. The quantity of any particular emotion appears to be just as important as the quality of it.

He lives on the theatrical stage, giving the impression that his entire life is a facade. His "as if" existence is annoying, because his lover simply can't touch the "real" him—the part of him that is most important. Rather than meaningful responses, the Non-Thinker gives knee-jerk reactions that are superficial and frustrating. Interestingly, if confronted with genuine feelings or observations, he shows surprise; he simply doesn't know that he is an actor in a play he had written years ago.

Ironically, the Non-Thinker is as ignorant about his feelings as the Obsessive Thinker is about his feelings. Asked how he feels, he might very well say, "I really don't know..." He might even be aware enough to tell us that his feelings are alien to him—that they come from someplace outside him and don't really belong to him at all. This makes it all the more difficult for his lover; if he doesn't own his feelings, then he certainly can't know what he genuinely feels about the people around him.

Not only does the Non-Thinker not understand his own emotions, he doesn't understand other people's emotions either. He may act "as if" he is angry or annoyed, but then becomes thoroughly confused when others respond to him in a like manner. He fails to notice that, although he experiences his behavior as play-acting, most other people really mean it when they become angry (sad, caring, etc.). His naiveté in these matters is almost beyond belief. Color his emotional climate "cold."

The Impulsive Thinker

Impulsive Thinkers and Non-Thinkers have something in common: they are both overwhelmed by their impulses. The Non-Thinker is stimulated by vivid, forceful impressions of a poorly organized world. The Impulsive Thinker is driven by whimsy, and by the feeling, "I just feel like doing it." Both types of Thinkers are passive recipients of a world filled with temptation—a world that seems to beckon them to react immediately with little regard to consequence.

The Impulsive Thinker is in fact a Non-Thinker who doesn't even enjoy the guidance of an "as if" existence. He doesn't act "as if" he is following a script, nor does he act "as if" he is pretending.

His impulses are pure. Life is simple: He wants it, he takes it. There is no intention or planning. There are few controls—either internal or external. There is just stimulation. His reactions are quick, abrupt, and ill conceived. If we listen carefully, we hear the Impulsive Thinker saying things like, "I don't know why I did it—I just did," or "I didn't mean to do it—it just happened," or perhaps "I didn't mean to do it—I just couldn't help myself."

The Impulsive Thinker's nature is characterized by whimsy and overwhelming urges. In his world, urges supplant reason and logic; stimulation replaces deliberateness and planning. We find these characteristics, in varying degrees, among many alcoholics, drug addicts, narcissists, and psychopathic personalities.

To a lesser degree, they appear in the behavior of most people who enjoy spontaneity. When coupled with internal controls (a conscience), whimsy and spontaneity lead to a joyous experience of life; without internal controls, they most often lead to unhappiness—especially for others.

Impulsive Thinkers give in to external pressure—whim, urge, or temptation. Something that they consider "out there" pulls them and "makes" them do things they know are not quite normal, but they do it anyway. The idea of will power or deliberation is foreign to them. That they themselves are responsible for their actions is likewise a foreign idea to them.

All of us experience the same kind of temptation—on occasion. What makes the Impulsive Thinker different is the degree and the percentage of time he is "tempted." We all are tempted to buy something we don't particularly need, but most of us won't grab a handbag or break the window of a jewelry store because we "just couldn't help it." Most of us won't go against the grain of social acceptability if it means ostracism. And most of us won't do it on a regular basis.

What sets the Impulsive Thinker apart from most people is his quick, unpredictable, and potentially dangerous behavior. Most of us enjoy whimsy within the context of a fairly stable lifestyle where one event follows another in a natural manner. The Impulsive Thinker's behavior, however, is generally erratic and poorly planned. His assessment of social rules and regulations is simply different and alien to most of us. For example, while most of us are willing to postpone immediate gratification ("I want what I want, but I'll wait a bit."), the Impulsive Thinker has little appreciation of the notion called "patience" or "delay." He takes what is offered, when it is offered: an unattended wallet, a "scam" promising much but delivering little, or any situation providing stimulation. His motto seems to be "Damn the torpedoes, full speed ahead," even when the course is fraught with danger for him or others.

What seems to be lacking is a concept of "worry." Unlike the Obsessive Thinker who worries constantly—who weighs and tries to balance all decisions—the Impulsive Thinker seldom shows concern about his choices. He seems to lack the voice (see "Voices of Passion") of an effectively critical parent who teaches a deep sense of morality and ethics. The result, in its most obvious form, is the relative ease with which the Impulsive Thinker lies, manipulates, and exhibits marked degrees of insincerity. These are the traits that make us crazy, and they are the very same traits that prevent long-term planning—planning that in many cases includes you, his lover.

The Obsessive Thinker, the Suspicious Thinker, the Non-Thinker, and the Impulsive Thinker represent personality styles that drive us to distraction. The Obsessive Thinker is always worrying, weighing consequences, while, at the same time, his communication is so vague and frustrating that we begin to avoid him. By the time he gets through assessing the details of details, searching for perfection, producing piles of paper at work, and ritualizing his behavior, we're ready to throw in the towel. After all, how much can we take? There is no humor to buffer reality, and little soul-mate communication to sustain the relationship. Obsessive Thinkers are not always unlovable. They often make for very tidy, well-meaning mates for people who can overlook their eccentricities.

The Suspicious Thinker is a bit more difficult to love. His groundless suspicions, his continuous search for trickery, his jealousy, and his possessiveness give us the feeling of being owned rather than being loved. But, then again, some people like that feeling! If his overly suspicious view of the world is not too severe, he can convince us his perceptions are accurate, and a tenuous but stable relationship is a possibility.

The Non-Thinker often can be quite appealing because of his impressionistic view of the world, his creative attempts at making sense out of it, and his tendency to be highly theatrical. His forgetfulness and lack of functional intelligence is often disregarded because of his charm, superficial sexiness, and the promise of excitement in the future. As the relationship matures, however, the absence of real intimacy becomes more apparent; and this lack of intimacy eats away at the relationship like termites on a succulent wood-frame house. The result, after a period of time, is a feeling of exhaustion and loneliness. Nonetheless, the Non-Thinker is often regarded as a sweet, naïve, zestful lover who commands our attention.

The Impulsive Thinker can also be lovable. He is unpredictable, exciting, whimsical, capricious, and—when he chooses to be—very attentive. If his impulsivity is not too severe, he conjures up a sense of adventure and mystery. Women addicted to "love" often find themselves involved with this kind of person, despite the absolute predictability of trouble in the future.

CHAPTER 10
CRAZY-MAKERS

Trouble in Paradise is often found among the Obsessive, the Suspicious, the Non-Thinking, and the Impulsive types. Their behaviors become so irritating and annoying, so critical and "paranoid," and so lacking in intimacy and commitment that living with him/her becomes a chore if not a burden. But they aren't the only difficult-to-get-along-with people out there. Eric Berne, a psychiatrist, and Virginia Satir, a family therapist, have documented a large variety other "Crazy-Makers" (reinterpreted to satisfy the theme of this book). To wit:

"The Trapper"

The "Trapper" is well known for his or her skill as a manipulator. He seduces us with his "helplessness," inviting us in to "save" him. Once we take the bait, he changes his helpless role. He becomes the aggressor, and we end up feeling embarrassed and foolish. More importantly, we end up wondering about our sanity. Here is a typical scenario: one partner tells the other he is tired of making all the decisions, and then he demands that she assume more responsibility. She does her best to relieve him of the burden. The first partner rejects not only the results of her efforts, but the effort itself. The same scene is played over and over and over again for years on end. The resultant anger, frustration, and feeling of betrayal are enough to make us swear off dating for months or years. "Trappers" are magnificently effective crazy-makers!

"The Double-Binder"

The "Double-Binder" has been implicated by many mental health specialists as a primary cause of emotional illness in children. The essential ingredient of the double bind is the "mixed message." The "Double-Binder" sends two communications, each one exclusive of the other. The husband says to his wife, for example, "The kids and I need you at home," and then goes on to suggest, "We need more money...you'll need to find a second job." Examples of this kind of crazy-making are numerous. Here's another instance: a mother tells her teenage daughter to eat everything on her plate, then comments negatively on the daughter's weight gain. Common responses to the double message are withdrawal, frustration, and regression. As the child becomes older, aggression and other kinds of "acting out" behaviors increase. The same responses occur in love relationships. Emotional climates become toxic. The "Double-Binder"—like all toxic personalities—should be studiously avoided.

The "Intimacy From Ten Feet Away" (IFTFA) Person

This crazy-maker pulls his lover in, while at the same time he pushes her away. Like the "Double-Binder," the IFTFA Person sends two messages, both equally strong. One message—often the verbal one—implies that the crazy-maker finds his lover attractive and wants her to share his physical and emotional boundaries. His lover, however, experiences something different: She experiences a rejection. The closer she tries to get, the harsher the rejection becomes. It is as though IFTFA Person wants to experience all the benefits of a love relationship without having to tolerate the presence of another human. The "Push-Pull" reflects a problem at the contact boundary. In its most severe form, the phenomenon takes on psychotic proportions. Fears of abandonment and intrusion on the part of the crazy-maker produce marked distortions of reality. Interestingly, despite the fact that the situation often is impossible to resolve, breaking away from IFTFA is extremely difficult because, like any true love addict, the IFTFA Person's lover convinces herself that maybe the "next time" he really will mean it when he says "I love you."

"The Whiner"

Male or female, the Whiner has the dubious distinction of being utterly objectionable within the first twenty minutes of meeting. His/her whining begins with a fingernails-on-the-chalk-board bleating about an octave higher than our comfort zone. S/he goes on and on...and on. The vocal qualities of the Whiner are simply dreadful. More repulsive, however, is his/her negativism, which reverberates through every word. The negativism has the power to bring us down, to dilute whatever happiness and joy we might be feeling at the time. It reminds us of a 3 AM feeding with a colicky infant who won't be satisfied no matter how much we coo and rock. The emotional climate created is a constant chill with no signs of a warming sun. We need only to count the number of hairs raised on the backs of our necks to discover how much we want to avoid a repeated encounter with the Whiner.

"The Armadillo"

The Armadillo buries himself with a seductive silence that leads us to presume competence. He doesn't let anyone in. He is armored, withholding, and tough. His boundaries are sacrosanct: There is a brightly lit sign over his head that says, "Do not tread on me." He presents himself as the strong silent type but, in truth, he is simply guarded and unwilling to share. He is often regarded as "mysterious"—a trait that is dangerously appealing to many women. It doesn't take long for us to realize that his strength is a sham. Once we get beyond the first layer of his personality, we learn there is no substance. But always there is a lingering doubt; we wonder what surprises he might have in store—if we only could break through the tough exterior. He is a crazy-maker because like the IFTFA he keeps us coming back even when we fully realize that the relationship will go nowhere. As far as the emotional climate goes: brrrr!

"The Possessor"

The Possessor is closely related to the Obsessive Thinker, on the one hand, and to the Suspicious Thinker, on the other. Feelings of closeness and devotion become fused with feelings of possessiveness and jealousy. He swings from despair to excitement and back again before we realize what is happening. He searches everywhere for assurance that his lover won't abandon him. He needs to know that she loves him, that she won't betray him. He needs to know that he is more important than the business meeting, a night out with the girls, or a visit to family in another state.

He reminds us of a three-year-old who clings to Mommy as she heads off to work. He also does something even more objectionable: he marks his partner with his scent so that other men will know who the real owner is. The "scent," of course, may take different forms: a costly gift, a special hair style, a tattoo, or he may even leave bits of his clothing at her apartment to remind her that she belongs only to him. By the time the Possessor's partner figures out what is really happening, it is almost too late; she has already been "owned." Despite this, the Possessor is extremely powerful. He is often exciting (when not depressed or angry) and attentive. If his partner can withstand the feeling of being trapped and she is as needy as the Possessor is, a caring albeit symbiotic relationship is possible. But for most of us, the Possessor is a crazy-maker who induces resentment, fear, and emotional withdrawal. The resulting emotional climate reminds us of a line in the old folk song, "Oh, Suzannah" ("...*the sun's so hot I froze to death...*").

Ann and Mike seemed to have a good time discussing these personality styles. Mike pointed out how his father had many of the characteristics of the Obsessive Thinker. His preoccupation with details, his moral judgments about the rectitude of certain religious, his philosophical convictions, and his indecisiveness despite strong opinions were all qualities that Mike could identify. Of course, Ann reminded him that he, Mike, often displayed the same behaviors.

Fortunately for both of them, Mike had a sense of humor and strong affection for Ann, who could melt his obsessive thoughts with a touch and a smile.

Ann also recognized her own tendency to behave in an obsessive fashion. She liked to connect the dots between real experiences and her fantasies; that, after all, was what her writing was all about, but she also liked the combination of strong impressions, the freedom to ooh and ahh at life's never-ending kaleidoscope of happenings, and her skill as a teller of stories. Mike said what he liked even more was her ability to balance her wonderful spontaneity with common sense. Here was one instance where the Obsessive Thinker and the Non-Thinker complemented each other's life style. The result was a sense of contentment and personal satisfaction. But, Mike wondered, if that was so, why wasn't he 100 percent sure that the relationship would work out? (Ann didn't remind him that Obsessive Thinkers always wonder that!)

To help Ann and Mike further understand the nature of emotional climates, I asked them to complete two separate scales. The first invoked their ability to spot "flat notes" in their relationship. The second involved their assessment of destructive behaviors that can and often do wreck relationships.

Here are the scales and the instructions:

Emotional Climate Scale

The 16 items on the scale below comprise a "thermometer" that measures the climate of your relationship. It asks you to judge how much of each personality or physical trait your partner exhibits at any particular time, and how much of each trait you find acceptable. There are two steps to the exercise:

Step 1: Place an "X" at the point on each scale that best describes how your partner behaves or presents himself.

Step 2: Underline an acceptable range for each characteristic. For example, let's rate three traits:

Emotional	1 2 3 4 5 X6 7	Unflappable
Serious	1 2 3 X4 5 6 7	Carefree
Shy	1 2 3 4 X5 6 7	Assertive

Here we find that the rater's partner is a fairly stable, a serious, and a somewhat shy person. What she feels most comfortable with, however, is a fairly stable, carefree, and somewhat bold person. In two out of three cases here, her partner falls outside the "emotional comfort" zone.

Complete the following scales in a similar fashion, and answer the questions that follow in order to assess the "emotional climate" of your relationship.

Joiner	1	2	3	4	5	6	7	Loner
Relaxed	1	2	3	4	5	6	7	Driven
Impulsive	1	2	3	4	5	6	7	Controlled
Secure	1	2	3	4	5	6	7	Worried
Blunt	1	2	3	4	5	6	7	Sophisticated
Shy	1	2	3	4	5	6	7	Assertive
Self-sufficient	1	2	3	4	5	6	7	Dependent
Trusting	1	2	3	4	5	6	7	Guarded
Practical	1	2	3	4	5	6	7	Capricious
Emotional	1	2	3	4	5	6	7	Unflappable
Earthy	1	2	3	4	5	6	7	Pretentious
Serious	1	2	3	4	5	6	7	Carefree
Lackadaisical	1	2	3	4	5	6	7	Disciplined
Reserved	1	2	3	4	5	6	7	Outgoing
Casual	1	2	3	4	5	6	7	Formal
Unattractive	1	2	3	4	5	6	7	Attractive

After you have identified where your partner lies along each scale, and you have underlined the "comfort zone" for each dimension, examine the scales where your partner falls outside your emotional comfort zone. How compatible is your desired "temperature" with the behavior of your lover?

Here is the profile that Ann produced when asked to complete the scale:

Joiner	1	2	3	4	5	6X	7	Loner
Relaxed	1	2	3	4	5	6X	7	Driven
Impulsive	1	2	3	4X	5	6	7	Controlled
Secure	1	2	3X	4	5	6	7	Worried
Blunt	1	2	3	4	5	6X	7	Sophisticated
Shy	1	2	3	4	5X	6	7	Assertive
Self-reliant	1	2	3X	4	5	6	7	Dependent
Trusting	1	2	3	4X	5	6	7	Guarded
Practical	1	2	3X	4	5	6	7	Capricious
Emotional	1	2	3	4	5	6	7X	Unflappable
Earthy	1	2	3	4	5	6X	7	Pretentious
Serious	1	2	3	4X	5	6	7	Carefree
Lackadaisical	1	2	3	4	5	6X	7	Disciplined
Reserved	1	2	3	4X	5	6	7	Outgoing
Casual	1	2	3	4	5	6X	7	Formal
Unattractive	1	2	3	4	5	6X	7	Attractive

Ann's ratings suggested that she and Mike were compatible in most of the areas measured. He tended to be more formal, less social, more practical, and a bit more reserved and conservative than she was. But, she also felt that he was extremely attractive and sexy, secure, sophisticated and self-sufficient, all qualities that she always regarded as essential for a relationship to work. Asked about the differences in their temperament, she summed up her feelings quickly: "That's why we're together…to balance each other." And that's why, she added, they wanted to stay together. For her, the emotional climate was perfect.

Mike's ratings were similar to Ann's. His range of comfort was comparable in most areas. Here's what his profile looked like:

Joiner	1	2	3X	4	5	6	7	Loner
Relaxed	1	2	3	4	5X	6	7	Driven
Impulsive	1	2	3X	4	5	6	7	Controlled
Secure	1	2	3X	4	5	6	7	Worried
Blunt	1	2	3	4	5	6X	7	Sophisticated
Shy	1	2	3	4	5	6X	7	Assertive
Self-reliant	1	2	3X	4	5	6	7	Dependent
Trusting	1	2X	3	4	5	6	7	Guarded
Practical	1	2	3	4	5	6X	7	Capricious
Emotional	1	2	3	4X	5	6	7	Unflappable
Earthy	1	2	3	4X	5	6	7	Pretentious
Serious	1	2	3	4	5X	6	7	Carefree
Disorderd	1	2	3	4	5X	6	7	Disciplined
Reserved	1	2	3	4	5	6X	7	Outgoing
Casual	1	2	3	4X	5	6	7	Formal
Unattractive	1	2	3	4	5	6X	7	Attractive

Mike's ratings on the Emotional Climate Scale pointed up the differences between the two people. Mike felt more comfortable with a reserved, practical-minded, less assertive, more controlled woman. That Ann did not satisfy these conditions was not a problem, however. She was beautiful, sophisticated, ambitious, self-directed, down-to-earth, and totally trusting. The areas where they appeared to be incompatible did not damage the relationship in the least. Ann provided Mike with humor, whimsy, a carefree attitude, sponta-neity, and, with her "joiner" orientation, further provided him with an entrée to various social and professional organizations. In short, they complemented or, perhaps more accurately, they completed each other.

Destructive Behavior

The emotional climate of a relationship is affected by many factors: different degrees of intimacy, passion, and commitment, different reasons for involvement, and different personality styles. Each source of incompatibility brings with it its own brand of emotional upheaval and emotional pressure systems, some less tolerable than others. But there are other reasons why people have trouble with the coupling process—less profound but surely as powerful. These include blatantly destructive habits, attitudes and behaviors.

The scales below describe a variety of troublesome behaviors and attitudes that play havoc with relationships. Ann and Mike were in the coupling phase, the third stage of the coupling process, a time when the weaknesses of a relationship are tested by time and experience. Mild cracks, slight flaws, in the relationship will be magnified and either accepted, rejected, or simply ignored. For example, the alcoholic, the pressure to impress his lover having been reduced, begins to drink a little more than before, waiting to see how his partner will react. An early and definitive rejection will drive the alcoholic to AA, to a psychotherapist, or to sobriety. A clear acceptance of the drinking will encourage more of the same in future years, a path appealing to some but not many. The same scenario applies to the gambler, the rage-aholic, the clingy person, or the depressed one. Within the suppression of a decisive response lie the seeds of despair, desperation, and—ultimately—destruction.

I asked Ann and Mike to complete the scale below as honestly as possible. I instructed them as follows: "Check the space under the number which best describes the degree to which each of the behaviors/attitudes/habits has damaged your relationship with your partner.

Destructive Behavior Scale

| Behavior | Not Damaging | | | Very Damaging |
	1	2	3	4
1. Disagreement over $	____	____	____	____
2. Gambling	____	____	____	____
3. Absence from Home	____	____	____	____
4. Initiation of Sex	____	____	____	____
5. Frequency of Sex	____	____	____	____
6. Quality of Sex	____	____	____	____
7. Unfaithfulness	____	____	____	____
8. Jealousy	____	____	____	____
9. Impotence/Frigidity	____	____	____	____
10. Alcohol/Drug Abuse	____	____	____	____
11. Temper Outbursts	____	____	____	____
12. Physical Abuse	____	____	____	____
13. Nagging	____	____	____	____
14. Poor Communication	____	____	____	____
15. Dependency/Parents	____	____	____	____
16. In-laws	____	____	____	____
17. No Mutual Interests	____	____	____	____
18. Selfishness	____	____	____	____
19. Clinginess	____	____	____	____
20. Lack of Friends	____	____	____	____
21. Child-Rearing Values	____	____	____	____
22. Different Religions	____	____	____	____
23. Lack of Trust	____	____	____	____
24. Lack of Respect	____	____	____	____
25. Political Differences	____	____	____	____

With the exception of item 25, Political Differences, neither Ann nor Mike could think of behaviors or attitudes that they considered "Damaging" to their relationship. Both endorsed item #25 as "Somewhat Damaging" because of their differences about politics. Mike was much more reserved in his willingness to support "Liberal" issues, such as Affirmative Action and trade agreements. Ann was a staunch supporter of the ERA and women's rights. But in these matters they agreed to disagree and always managed to go to bed without any lingering anger toward the other party. Had they endorsed three or more "Extremely Damaging" items or five or more "Somewhat Damaging" items, their relationship would be too painful to endure, and the likelihood of their staying together would have been remote. The wind-chill factor in such cases produces an emotional climate cold enough to cause frostbite. There are tens of thousands of couples that subject each other to any number of these emotional assaults, and many of the relationships endure despite them. Perhaps this was the primary reason for the development of the field of couple's and marriage counseling, and the reason why it so often fails.

By establishing an internal yardstick to measure whether the emotional climate of their relationship was "too hot," "too cold," or "just right," Ann and Mike became more convinced than ever that their love was real. By establishing an internal yardstick to measure the emotional climate of relationships, most of us could avoid becoming "crazy" with anger, sadness, and frustration.

CHAPTER 11
IN THE MOOD FOR LOVE?

A nn and Mike had explored three basic questions: (1) Were they compatible as lovers? (2) Were their motivations for coupling authentic and mutual? and (3) Was the emotional climate of their relationship comfortable—or at least tolerable? The answers to these three basic questions affirmed what they had already suspected: they were "really truly in love." Ann felt more secure about where the relationship was heading. Mike felt less pressure about committing himself to the relationship.

When we began the course of counseling, Ann and Mike had four choices available to them: they could terminate, maintain, expand, or limit the time they spent with each other. Now they had tentatively decided to expand it. However, their education about themselves and about each other was only partially complete.

Ann and Mike were attempting to set up standards. They wanted to know whether they matched each other's personality profile. Each one had checked off a laundry list of "Is s/he or isn't s/he?" or "Does s/he or doesn't s/he?" type of questions. Quietly, they tested each other's perception of the world. Was Mike too (in)tense? Or, was he a bit too casual? Would Ann be too dependent, or would her behavior fall within the emotional comfort zones that Mike had established years before? By the time they completed their assessments, they would have established personal profiles revealing—all things being equal—whether they could fit comfortably into each other's life.

Ann and Mike spent many hours exploring who they were and how they wanted their relationship to develop. On several occasions, Ann pointed out that Mike could be grouchy and irritable. Mike in turn pointed out that Ann withdrew and seemed to be resentful whenever he left her. Ann admitted that although Mike and she were not living together, she became pouty when she saw him packing his bags after a wonderful weekend together. Changes in mood became a major topic of discussion for several sessions.

I explained the basic premise. We wake up in the morning, and we go to sleep at night. In between, we experience a stream of awareness, perceptions, emotions, and external behaviors, many of which can be grouped together to form various rituals, pastimes, hobbies, work activities, and play activities.

The outcome of each of these events is predictable. For example, one common "ritual" is greeting someone. The greeting ritual proceeds in a well-defined order: the first "hello" is followed by "how are you? (the family, the children, the new job, etc.)," and is eventually followed by "goodbye." "Going to Work" consists of a long series of activities which might include awakening at a particular time, performing multiple sub-activities such as showering, grooming, dressing, eating breakfast, riding to work and engaging in specific work activities, and then leaving for home.

The events flow simultaneously and sequentially from morning to night. Some of the events are planned; some are spontaneous. Sequences of behaviors, taken together, define what we call a "lifestyle."

We can apply same idea to emotions. We wake up with an emotion, perhaps one left over from a dream or from an encounter the evening before. This emotion is followed by another emotion, which is followed by yet another, and so forth. Generally, these emotions are consistent with each other and with our overt behavior. If they are not, there is a problem. For example, some angry people act "sweet", but intuitively we sense that they are seething. Some people laugh a bit too often and a bit too loudly and then suddenly become sad and depressed. These people confuse us and put us on our guard.

How well our emotions flow along and correlate with the way we behave is important because significant discrepancies serve as danger signals. For example, angry feelings are most often followed by withdrawal, disgust, resentment, and vindictiveness. If anger turns into rage and vindictiveness immediately, there is a real danger of emotional or physical assault. If a resentful person is unable to express his resentment directly, s/he may express it indirectly ("Oh, I'm sorry. I didn't mean to step on your toe."), causing annoyance and withdrawal. Most commonly, however, there is a natural resolution of feelings within a short period of time. The angry person expresses his anger in an appropriate and effective fashion; the resentful person finds a way of expressing his resentment more directly; and the depressed person screws up enough courage to fight off overwhelming discouragement and go on with life.

Several of the major mood chains are offered here as examples of how emotions change—or fail to change—over the course of time. Learning the subtleties of emotional change helped Ann and Mike examine dominant moods, mood sequences, and their influences on their relationship.

The Anger Sequence

The Anger Sequence begins with anger, which is then followed by a sequence of emotions: withdrawal, disgust, resentment, and vindictiveness. In the emotionally healthy person, the sequence resolves itself quickly and predictably. The most effective resolution comes in the form of the direct expression our anger. People who cannot express the anger directly may need to use unconscious adaptive maneuvers such as repression or denial—not the best way to resolve the problem, but often the only way under certain circumstances. For example, expressing our annoyance with our boss might not be in our best interest, so we have to swallow hard and subdue the emotion using whatever defenses we have available to us.

In many cases, however, the Anger Sequence doesn't resolve itself, and we find ourselves ruminating about the event. Obsessive and Suspicious Thinkers carry the thoughts around with them day and night until they can figure out how shake them off. Impulsive Thinkers might take short cuts to resolution and simply act out their anger/rage without regard to consequence or propriety. Unfinished feelings demand completion: joy demands a feeling of light-heartedness, depression demands withdrawal, sadness demands tears, and anger demands physical and/or verbal release.

In the Anger Sequence, if the natural flow of feelings is blocked from completion, the sequence of emotions reverses itself. In the usual sequence, anger precedes withdrawal which precedes disgust which precedes resentment and vindictiveness. However, when the normal sequence is disrupted, the sequence of feelings reverses itself, and resentment/vindictiveness leads to disgust which leads to withdrawal and then to anger. Unless the sequence can be terminated, the sequence reverses itself again and again until either through fatigue, distraction, or resolution, the sequence is abandoned.

Oddly, while much has been written about emotions, little has been written about the obvious fact that feelings follow a more or less prescribed course. Why one emotion follows another remains a mystery. In part, the answer lies in each person's unique body chemistry and genetic make-up. In part, a feeling such as withdrawal serves as a natural protective response to anger because (1) it protects us from further emotional disorganization (anxiety) and (2) it protects other people from the harmful effects of our temper outbursts.

Coming out of withdrawal, it makes a great deal of biological sense for a person to go into a short period of disgust, because with disgust comes a kind of emotional vomiting that helps the body rid itself of the initial toxic event (thought, picture, behavior). The emergence of resentment and vindictiveness appears to have some utility in that it allows us to keep the toxic event at arm's length until the matter is ready to be resolved. The Anger Sequence, then, goes something like this:

ANGER-- > WITHDRAWAL-- > DISGUST-- > RESENTMENT--> VINDICTIVENESS-- > (RESOLUTION?)

So far, so good. The effective Anger Sequence works to discharge bad feelings and, to that extent, it has survival value. The question is whether the sequence is timely and consistent. By timely, we refer to the recession of feelings within a reasonable and "healthy" period of time; by consistent, we refer to the predictable sequencing of emotions each time the initial feeling (e.g. rage, anger, sadness, depression, euphoria) is fired off.

Problems with either the timeliness or the consistency of a mood chain will mean problems in a relationship. If lovers are unable to discharge feelings of anger or rage in a timely fashion, the chances they will end up being very unhappy. Verbal or physical violence and/or the wanton destruction of property may follow. People who have not discovered a way to effectively discharge and resolve the Anger Sequence over an extended period of time often are the very same people who end up in prisons, hospitals, or in doctors' offices.

Each of us can get caught up in a particular phase of the Anger Sequence. If we become stuck in the "withdrawal" phase of the sequence, for instance, we will come across as depressed, unfeeling and uncommunicative. People will not be able to touch us with either words or hugs, and may eventually give up the effort. Again, if the withdrawal phase persists for a long time, especially if the original triggering event took place when we were very young, the mood chain may lead to severe regression, the safety of hospitalization, or to life as a recluse.

Disgust, if protracted, may lead to cynicism, pessimism, and malcontent. We experience "Disgusted" people as bitter and cynical people who dampen the spirit of fun and goodwill. They are "toxic" in the sense that we feel drained and tense even after a few minutes with them.

Likewise, if someone becomes fixated on resentment/vindictiveness, people around him walk away sensing something is "missing." The contact may be sharp, but the connection is weak, even though the resentful person wears a smile.

We want to emphasize that each of these emotions is not destructive in and of itself. Only when they fail to dissipate in a timely fashion, or when they become unpredictable do they cause problems for us and for the people around us.

The Humiliation Sequence

As seen in the following sequence, Humiliation becomes troublesome because it is so closely tied up with shame and feelings of inferiority:

HUMILIATION / SHAME / INFERIORITY--> FEAR--> HOPELESSNESS--> ISOLATION--> AGITATION--> RESTLESSNESS--> FRUSTRATION--> ANGER --> WITHDRAWAL --> DISGUST--> RESENTMENT--> VINDICTIVENESS--> (RESOLUTION?)

This sequence may take many days, many months, or even years to resolve itself, because each emotion is so strong and so difficult to complete. A feeling of Humiliation/Shame/Inferiority is all too easily reactivated in all of us. We need only to reach back to our experiences as a child: the first time we had a toileting accident or got caught with our hand in the proverbial cookie jar. Or, more meaningfully, as an adult, the time we made a "fool" of us at the office party, or perhaps the time we exposed our thoughts, feelings, or nakedness to someone who rejected us outright, leaving us feeling too small to fight back.

Each emotion in this sequence plays a role in helping us regain our emotional equilibrium. We begin by feeling small and weak. We then become frightened and we either try to distance ourselves from the humiliating person (event), or we try to appease him/her. Next comes a period of hopelessness. We don't know what to do so we withdraw and isolate ourselves. After a period of time in isolation, we begin the process of reintegration, the first stage of which is much internal restlessness, experienced as irritation and agitation.

This leads to attempts to change our situation, which in turn leads to feelings of frustration.

Frustration may lead to aggression, anger, or, if it is very great, to regression. Regression is the act of returning to a stage of behavior that has been "successful" in the past (tantrum behavior, poutiness, passivity). If we work through these emotional states, we experience growth, and that is what is most interesting. Without frustration, there is no growth. Ironically, if the frustration is too great, there also is no growth.

Infants fall down many times before they learn to walk. Kindergarten students learn to read only by making many mistakes and accepting correction. The temporary frustrations in both cases lead to growth. But, let's say we want a parent's attention, and our fictional parent cannot or will not give us the attention we want no matter how much we ask, plead, or display our temper. We are then left with a hole in our personality—a blind spot—that prevents our selves from ripening into mature adults. Years later we may find us sitting on the counselor's sofa, wondering why we can't feel closer to our lover or spouse or children—or anyone else for that matter.

Clearly, if the Humiliation/Shame/Inferiority Sequence is triggered many times before it is resolved, our perception of the world will be affected, and eventually the way we react to the people around us will be affected. Is it any wonder that wo/men in abusive (humiliating) relationships become so confused and hopeless that their perception of who they are becomes so distorted?

The Failure Sequence

Here's another sequence, the Failure Sequence, all too common among couples who complain of failed attempts at establishing personal relationships:

FEELINGS OF FAILURE-->FEELINGS OF SELF-DENIGRATION--> ISOLATION --> (RESOLUTION?)

The Failure Sequence begins with the feeling we have somehow disappointed someone. We perceive ourselves as inadequate and incompetent. If these feelings are turned inward, there is self-denigration, depression, and withdrawal. Of course, the feelings can be turned outward as well, and, instead of we feeling small and incompetent, we project the "holes" in our personality onto the environment (most often the people we love or the people we hate). If incompetence is one of those "holes," we begin to see "incompetence" in our lover, our boss, our best friend, our worst enemy, or anyone else who has absorbed our interest. It is they who are inept, not we. If this kind of thinking is carried to an extreme, we begin to develop delusions about our power *vis á vis* the power of the people around us. Suspicious thinking follows in short order.

Depending on the nature of our (or our lover's) personality structure, failure will trigger either subtle forms of panic/resignation or temper/rage. The resolution in either case requires a realistic assessment of who we are, what our weaknesses are, and what we can do about them. If we are able to overcome the failure and the resulting frustration, we become stronger; we become the heroes of life. If we are not able to overcome the failure, we (and our lover) will become increasingly more withdrawn or tempestuous, and—more often than not—dour, defensive, and combative.

The Addiction Sequence

This chapter would not be complete without a consideration of another sequence, the Addiction Sequence, an increasingly common condition in which the "love addict" finds the relationship burdensome and self-destructive, yet feels powerless to end it. To say that the addicted partner "loves too much" is a simplification of the real problem, which may be that s/he doesn't know how to love at all.

A mature love relationship, by definition, requires reciprocity. We give and we receive according to our energy and our needs, but always there is a mutually agreed-upon give and take. In the case of an addictive love, the relationship swings rapidly and erratically; the see-saw affection is never quite balanced, and frustration, panic, and anger displace the playful, mildly exhilarating, smoothly coordinated exchanges of passion and intimacy we have come to expect in healthy relationships.

The Addiction Sequence is particularly difficult because, despite the pain, the addicted lover doesn't want to give it up. She denies, she represses, and she rationalizes. In short, she does whatever she has to do to push distress out of conscious awareness. Invariably, with time, the relationship becomes worse: tension and stress increase; satisfaction and happiness decrease.

Nonetheless, the addict of love holds onto her relationship with the tenacity of a child who senses she is about to be abandoned. Catastrophic expectations set off a chain reaction of behaviors and moods that have the same intensity we find in the alarming behavior of alcoholics and drug addicts who have been cut off from their supplies. The destructive nature of the addiction becomes apparent as we consider the ongoing, increasingly debilitated condition of the addict over time. Comparisons between an addictive process and a disease process are common; and they are not without foundation.

Love addicts learn their lessons from unhealthy family relationships long before a particular "love" relationship actually begins. The sequence seems to begin innocently enough when the addict is asked to assume too much responsibility for the happiness or contentment of a chronically ill member of her family, often an alcoholic parent. The responsibility calls for total control over a situation where total control is impossible. With the investment of time and energy, a state of dependency develops, and, after many years, becomes crystallized. The question, of course, is who becomes dependent on whom?

The answer is that the caretaker (addict) and the patient (family member) depend on the other. A symbiotic relationship has been created: one cannot exist without the other without severely damaging the by-now-accepted delicate balance within the relationship. The result of this misaligned alliance is a skewed view of the world and, more relevant, a skewed view of love relationships.

The love addict either creates—or searches for—a relationship that mimics what s/he has become accustomed to: a relationship with a dependent, unhappy, and needy wo/man. Perversely, the key to the relationship is not "being happy," or "being adored," or "being comfortable." The key to the relationship is trying—trying to please, trying to cure, and trying to control. The addiction is not to love per se, or even to the other person: the addiction is to the feeling that historically came along with love, a feeling called trying.

Here, then, is the Addiction Sequence:

NEED FOR CONTROL ("TRIES" TO LOVE, "TRIES" TO KEEP LOVER HAPPY)—> GUILT / ANGER / FRUSTRATION ("TRIES" TO CONTROL -AGAIN) —> "TRIES TO TALK ABOUT IT" (GUILT / ANGER / FRUSTRATION)—>FEELINGS OF FAILURE (EXCUSES TO FRIENDS AND FAMILY)—>WITHDRAWAL (IRRATIONAL FEARS AND ANGER)—> OBSESSION WITH CONTROL —>FAILURE —>ATTEMPTS TO ESCAPE (BECOMES WORKAHOLIC, ALCOHOLIC, DRUG ADDICT AND / OR SUICIDAL)—>BOTTOMS OUT (ADMITS DEFEAT)—> SEEKS HELP (AA, GROUP THERAPY) ....(REBIRTH OF OWN INTERESTS AND SPONTANEITY)

The Addiction Sequence is a complicated and an extremely long sequence. It takes many months, and perhaps many years to complete. Many addicts never complete it. In essence, it begins with the need for control (a need that is foisted upon the addict) and ends with rebirth (a need generated by the will to survive). "Trying" to make the partner happy leads to "trying" to control, then to "guilt / frustration / anger," which then leads to obsessive "need to control ", and to self-destruction or (hopefully) rebirth.

It is difficult to find any room for respite in such a sequence of behaviors and moods. The love addict struggles to establish equilibrium within herself as well as between herself and her lover. Failure to achieve a proper balance produces a protracted state of emotional crisis in both parties.

People who struggle with uncompleted emotional sequences experience increased stress at all levels: physical, emotional, intellectual, and behavioral.

Emotional Symptoms

Anxiety, fear, and depression dominate the mood of the addicted lover. The message behind her frequent decrease in sex drive and apathy is insecurity. Loss of control, anger, frustration, and hopelessness occur all too often. Sleeplessness, emotional sensitivity, uncommunicativeness, and fatigue are the symptoms that most physicians hear about when the addict schedules her next physical examination.

Cognitive Deficiencies

The addict's thinking is fuzzy, disorganized, forgetful, and lacking in vigilance. The body's lack of harmony is evident: concentration is poor, speech is pressured, and judgment becomes impaired.

Behavioral Symptoms

The addict lover experiences abrupt changes in habits: her exercise regimen is decreased along with her ability to relax. Sugar and fat intake increases, and, ironically, so does the use of drugs (smoking, alcohol). Irritability, querulousness, and discouragement become the bases for relationships at home and often at work.

* * *

While all moods have beginning points and ending points, the Anger, Humiliation, Failure, and Addictive Sequences appear to be the ones with the most potential for harming our relationships. Life with our lover becomes easier if we understand mood chains, and the "rules" governing them.

Mood Processes

Emotions follow a specified course that, under normal circumstances, is relatively permanent. We only need to study the sequence, and the duration of our lover's mood phases, to get a rough idea of how life will be in the future. If, for example, our lover becomes enraged, and this mood lasts for three days before slipping into withdrawal, the chances are that this will be the mood pattern in the future.

It takes a certain amount of patience, stamina, and generosity to tolerate three days of anger/rage. Our job, of course, is to discover whether we can realistically handle this kind of emotional reactivity on our lover's part. Clearly, our assessment should include a consideration of our own mood, and the sequences they follow: How do we respond to our lover's anger/rage/withdrawal? How long does it take us to run through our mood chains?

I remember clearly when I first became interested in mood processes and how emotions resolve themselves. Connie, a thirty-four-year-old secretary, sought counseling because a fellow she had been dating for about six months suddenly had become withdrawn, uncommunicative, and uncharacteristically forgetful about social engagements. Finally, after many weeks of emotional turmoil, Connie discovered that Charles had become involved with another woman.

She became enraged, and by the time she came to see me, she had become so overwhelmed by feelings of anger and betrayal, she was beginning to "feel crazy." She was concerned, she said, because she felt she was neglecting her young son. As we continued to talk about her feelings, it became clear to Connie she had always had a difficult time with anger and disappointment. What usually happened was this: she would withdraw to her room for two days while the rage passed into disgust, a feeling she didn't enjoy because people wanted to avoid her. Fortunately, the disgust phase would pass quickly—generally after a day or two—and Connie would become a bit more sociable. Resentment, however, had always been a problem for her. It seemed to hang on forever. No matter how much she rationalized the situation, no matter how much she resolved to be "more understanding" or "more patient," the resentment stuck to her like two-sided adhesive tape.

Exploring the resentment and its ultimate "payoff," Connie found that at some level she actually enjoyed her feelings of resentment and vindictiveness. They gave her the opportunity to feel self-righteous—and it validated her as the victim of the situation. Once Connie understood the sequence of her moods and how long each phase would endure, she was able to teach her son how to deal with her moodiness. The disappointment with Charles continued to nag her, but she finally understood that with time her feelings would resolve themselves, and that she wouldn't be "crazy" forever, a fear that she had harbored even as a child.

Uniqueness

Each person's unique biology and early teachings limit the number and quality of mood sequences. Some people are more complicated than others. Conversely, some people seem to experience few emotions or moods. In either case, biological make-up and genetic disposition appear to play major roles in the production of mood sequences; early teachings account for the rest.

How we feel and behave influences the behavior of the people around us. For example, the behavior of children who don't seem to have the "genes" for remorse will elicit more intense discipline from frustrated and frightened parents than the behavior of children who are more compliant.

Likewise, research tells us that "neurotic" people experience stress for longer periods of time than do "normal" people. In one study, for example, a group of neurotic individuals and a group of normal people were compared on a number of physiological measures. Both groups were exposed to the sound of a gunshot. While both groups reacted immediately and intensely to the noise, the neurotic group took much longer to return to a normal baseline of physiological reactivity. Other studies strongly point to innate differences in temperament as a major reaction to stress.

Individual Differences

Each mood follows a standard course, which differs from person to person in intensity and quality. When you think back to your experiences with old friends, family, and lovers, you can begin to appreciate that each person has a certain "personality" that makes him different from others. For some people, an angry feeling is followed by withdrawal; for others, it is followed by a disquieting calm. For still others, it is followed by a temper outburst, quickly resolved and quickly forgotten. Each of us differs in the way our feelings evolve and finally resolve themselves. The sequence of emotions is our own in terms of duration and quality.

Unfinished Feelings

Disrupting the normal course of a mood sequence often leads to an exacerbation of the specific mood disrupted. Blocking the angry feeling leads to more anger; blocking the feeling of withdrawal leads to more withdrawal; and blocking the feeling of humiliation leads to even more humiliation. Each feeling has a prescribed course and duration, and these have to be respected. Time and patience are needed to allow a person to complete his sequence of feelings. The natural occurrence of events needs to flow freely. And this requires we understand how people operate and how not to take it personally when we inadvertently interfere with the resolution of a sequence of emotions.

The interruption of a mood sequence leads to behavior reflecting the nature of the blocked mood as well as a general feeling of "incompleteness." We have all experienced "saying the wrong thing at the wrong time." Someone we care about (and perhaps love) is angry, and we try to be helpful by being clever or witty. The next thing we know there is a blast of cold air that sends us cowering to the next room. We call our best friend and ask, "What did I do wrong?" Our friend, if he is wise, says, "Don't worry. You just caught her at a bad time. It'll blow over. Just give it time." Similarly, with kindness and affection, we may say to the person caught up in one of the phases of the Humiliation/Shame/Inferiority Sequence, "It's not your fault, you just did what you thought was right." And the person, instead of feeling relieved, becomes even more withdrawn, and even more isolated.

Each mood or sequence may be slowed or quickened through therapeutic intervention, but the sequence itself follows a prescribed course. By "therapeutic intervention," we don't necessarily mean psychotherapy. A therapeutic intervention could be a vacation, the adoring arms of a son or daughter around our waists, a call from an old friend, or an act of kindness by a stranger. Disgust melts with honesty and truth. Anger dissipates with affection. Humiliation is lessened with self-forgiveness. The sequence of emotions still runs its course, but the course is shortened, often dramatically so.

Free-flowing mood sequences are subjectively experienced as a feeling of well-being and self-control. When we block the natural flow of emotions (or allow our lover to do so) we feel tense and unfulfilled. With the blockage of a sequence of moods comes the frustration of feeling "unfinished"; and this leads to an irrepressible desire to complete the emotional sequence once and for all. On the other hand, when a sequence is experienced completely, we return to a feeling that the "unfinished business" has been completed, and that we are whole again. Psychotherapy may be beneficial in instances where the mood chains are not free flowing. Its role, in this regard, is not to "cure" the individual, but to help the patient loosen the emotional logjams that will facilitate the completion of the emotional sequence.

Flow of Energy

The blockage in a particular mood sequence is experienced as "numbness," "emotional death," or "dread" (Angst). Mood chains are made up of different moods that merge imperceptibly into each other until an emotional sequence is completed. This requires a flowing of energy. When the flow of energy is blocked or interrupted, we experience an "emotional death" or numbness. We need only to recall a time when we became immobilized by trauma to realize how strongly such a blockage affects us. Subjectively, we feel an all-pervasive sense of dread—a combined state of paralysis and panic.

For example, if an Anger Sequence is triggered by a betrayal of someone we love, the normal sequence of moods includes anger, withdrawal, disgust, resentment, and vindictiveness and the resolution. Getting to the point of the resolution, however, requires that we work through the anger and the other disruptive emotions. If we fail to sense movement or progress, we begin to experience emotional stupefaction; and we begin to dread the future. The dread—panic plus paralysis—colors our perception of everything around us. The world is not safe; wo/men cannot yet be trusted; we become hypervigilant, suspicious, and easily startled. We interpret our environment through a filter made up of blocked emotions and numbness. We cannot free ourselves to enter a new relationship because we have not yet completed the last one.

If a blocked emotion cannot be loosened up through our own natural ability to reorganize our affective (emotional) life or through the interventions of a change agent (psychotherapist, physician, clergy, son/daughter, lover, change of environment), the internal numbness we feel may very well be expressed externally through acts of self-destruction, or, in some cases, through violence. This is one of the reasons why involvement with someone on the "rebound,"— someone who has not fully worked through feelings of loss—is emotionally so dangerous. Those of us who are sensitive to feelings of rejection vow never to get involved with such people.

Of course, there is another perspective. This requires that we appreciate the nature of our candidate-lover's dilemma, give him time, and make auspicious interventions of kindness, concern, and attention. If, despite our good intentions, our lover continues to remain "numb," it is perhaps best to part—at least for a while—and to allow the emotional forces to continue to unfold in their own fashion. The rule of thumb is this: provide gentle encouragement twenty times—the normal rate for learning. If our lover doesn't "get it," we need to free ourselves to look elsewhere, and to free our lover so he can work through the blocked feelings.

Confusion

The feeling we call "confusion" is the result of several incongruous mood sequences fired off simultaneously. This is most apparent in abusive relationships, or in situations where there is "co-dependency." If our lover were consistently mean-spirited, destructive and deceptive, we could respond with clear and pure anger. The matter would be resolved quite quickly. We get tripped up, however, because often in addition to anger, our spouse evokes some other feeling—concern, caring or sweetness. We find ourselves feeling confused instead of angry although the reasons for our anger are reasonable.

This may be a sign that our lover is a skillful manipulator of feelings and thoughts. More often, however, the confusion erupts because he presents a genuinely mixed picture of behaviors: nastiness/destructiveness/hurtfulness plus sweetness/carelessness/ignorance. Part of us responds with the anger/rage sequence, while another part responds with a caring/love sequence of emotions. We feel confused because we are confused. The emotional sequences are incompatible; our bodies reflect the incompatibility with tears and clenched fists; our minds reflect the incompatibility with confusion.

Confusion is a signal that there is something very wrong with the emotional exchange between our lover and us. If it occurs too often, it augers ill for the future, and it is best not to linger.

Mood Sequences in Real Life

Ann and Mike seemed to be doing well. They freely discussed their concerns about the future. In the early spring, they reported that they had spent three days together on Plum Island, a small island off the north shore of Massachusetts, where Ann often spent time on weekends. The days were filled with walks on the beach, the evenings with loving and laughing. But now it was time for Ann's return to Boston and for Mike's return to England.

On the way home, the couple had stopped at P.J.'s, a convenience store, so that Ann could have a final word with Jane, the proprietor. She told Jane, "It was wonderful! Mike is everything I ever dreamed he would be. He loves me! I can't think of anything that could keep us apart."

Ann recalled that the drive to back to Boston seemed to take forever. She had felt an odd mixture of exhilaration and sadness, excitement mixed with fear. Mike, she observed, was quiet. On his part, Mike recalled that he and Ann were both experiencing a sense of profound loss.

As Ann recounted the story, she noted that about twenty miles from Boston, she suddenly felt insecure. She asked, "Where do we go from here, Mike? You know I loved the time we spent together. You seem so quiet, so detached—have I done anything wrong?" Mike didn't respond at all, and Ann began to think that Mike hadn't heard a thing she had said.

Ann laughed as she recalled thinking, "Typical male!"

Her voiced softened as she remembered Mike turning to her and, placing his hand over hers and squeezing it gently, said, "Ann, I love you very much."

Ann's hurt dissolved. In its place came confusion. What was she supposed to say now? She decided to remain quiet and to let Mike lead the conversation.

Miles passed. The farmland surrounding Newburyport gave way to the tree-lined highways, to the ubiquitous shopping centers, and then, finally, to the skyscrapers of Boston. Mike had remained quiet throughout the fifty-minute drive, and Ann had let him keep his emotional distance, telling herself that his behavior was sadness cloaked with aloofness.

I asked Ann and Mike if they could spot the changes in each other's moods as time wore on. Ann responded that she had seen Mike's visage change with each mile. First, there was withdrawal, then she saw his mouth turned down at the corners, and then his eyebrows arched. Then there was a sigh, and then he touched her hand again. Each emotion lasted only a minute or two and then merged imperceptibly into the next one. The sequence was completed by the time they reached Ann's condo in Boston. Despite Mike's silence, Ann recalled how deeply touched she was by his gentleness and the feeling of sadness she (correctly) guessed troubled Mike as he prepared for his trip across the Atlantic.

Mike reported that the emptiness of the apartment was palpable. Ann's sons hadn't yet returned from the visit with their father. He could no longer hide behind the isn't-the-landscape-beautiful as an excuse for the lack of conversation.

Ann remembered pouring two drinks, and, handing him one of them, she sat down next to him. She remembered thinking that Mike's eyes seemed to have lost their sparkle. "Mike," she said gently, "what's wrong...what are you thinking?"

Then—as Ann recalled the incident—the most romantic scene unfolded before her. Mike looked into her eyes. He smiled the same smile Ann saw the first time they had met. "Ann," she remembered him saying, "what is wrong is I don't want to leave you now or ever." He sipped his drink, never letting his eyes wander from her. "I need to hear you say that you will marry me as soon as I can settle my affairs back home."

These were the words she had waited months to hear, but now that it happened, she was confused. She told him, "Mike, I want that more than anything. But are you sure? We haven't spent a lot of time together really. Don't you think we need to wait?"

Mike remembered his response to her: "No, I don't think we should wait. I love you and I want to spend the rest of my life with you."

I urged Ann to remember the changes in her mood just as she clearly remembered the minute changes in Mike's mood.

"My breathing quickened and my heart began to pound. I was becoming very confused and nervous. I wondered: What is this feeling I'm feeling right now? Was it love? Panic? Perhaps both!"

What Ann felt were emotions that were (con)fused. Telling where one feeling leaves off and the next one begins is difficult. This is truer for some mood sequences than others. For example, the Humiliation sequence described above clusters feelings of humiliation, shame, and inferiority together, and while each of these feelings is experienced differently, the differences are subtle and hard to define. The other components of the sequence, however, are relatively easy to spot: fear and hopelessness along with liberal doses of isolation, agitation, frustration and anger. At the end of the sequence we generally find feelings of resentment and vindictiveness, often not expressed because of the very first feelings of the sequence, that is, inferiority and shame.

To dramatize this point, I asked Ann to recall her first marriage, a time when she had experienced, by her own admission, extreme feelings of inferiority. Tentatively, she remembered how her husband let her know indirectly and sometimes not so indirectly how dependent and silly she was. By the end of the first year of marriage, she had become frightened, discouraged, hopeless, and finally ended up barricading herself for days at a time in her bedroom. (They slept in separate bedrooms because, as her husband was sure to tell her on a regular basis, there was no need to sleep together if she couldn't handle the simple act of sexual gratification.) After months of being bashed, Ann became increasingly agitated and frustrated. She still had enough of her self-esteem left intact to know that she could not go on this way. At first, she began to show her anger passively: she neglected the wash, the cooking and the housekeeping for days on end. But her attempts to express her anger left her feeling so helpless that she withdrew even more. Looking back on it, she recalled feeling that she had to isolate herself almost completely to keep from committing acts of violence either to her husband, to herself, or to both. Eventually Ann sought out a psychiatrist who was wise enough to spot a potentially serious problem and who hospitalized Ann briefly for depression.

In the hospital, Ann attended group therapy and began to gain the confidence she needed in order to break away from the untenable relationship with her emotionally abusive husband. Her experience in the hospital also taught her something even more important, that her feelings, however nasty they were, would pass if given enough time, and if she had the courage to seek assistance. Her feelings of shame and inferiority were old feelings learned before she could walk or talk. It was now time that she re-decide those early decisions about her worthiness, to learn how to become aware of her feelings of anger and frustration and withdrawal and to accept them knowing that they would pass in time.

Her need to vindicate herself came in the form of an excellent divorce attorney who was able to secure a generous settlement on Ann's behalf. The last words Ann heard from her estranged husband after the legal proceedings were: "But why didn't you tell me?"

Ann laughed as she recalled how completely out of touch her husband had been. "Not that he was a bad man," she told Mike and me, "he was just so self-absorbed. And that's why it's so important for me to know that Mike's trouble with commitment won't turn me into an emotional vegetable again."

Mike's response? He picked up Ann's hand and kissed it gently, all the while looking so deeply into her eyes that she actually began to swoon.

Like Ann and Mike, we all need to re-learn how we experience our partner's feelings. While Ann, confronted with Mike's tendency to withdraw, let the situation ride until a more propitious moment arrived, Mike was less sensitive. Nonetheless, he appreciated her efforts to make contact with him. This is the very essence of the coupling process: to communicate with our lover within a sphere of comfort and safety.

Ann's feelings of nervousness and Mike's longing to be with her had propelled them into a mad dash for counseling. Their feelings were powerful and needed to be resolved before the final step—marriage—could be taken. Again, they reassured me that they truly loved each other and they were convinced that working on the issues centering on intimacy would not take long. I believed them. But I also realized that there were a number of other questions that needed to be asked and answered.

Being able to predict the behaviors or feelings of our partner provides us with consistency and with a certain degree of control, both of which make difficult emotional encounters tolerable. We often say that someone is a "grouch" or "depressed" or "bitter." What we don't seem to understand too well is that these mood states don't last forever or, conversely, that they can dominate the emotional life of some of us for hours, days, or, in unusual instances, even for months and years. There are individuals who cannot (biologically) or who will not (psychologically) relinquish certain moods, and who will remain fixed permanently in a particular emotional state.

We often don't understand how our lover experiences his inner world at any given moment. Therefore, we fail to appreciate there are times when it is better to keep our distance and to be quiet rather than to barge into his privacy. At such times, we need to learn to be patient, to learn when our partner is approachable, and to learn what kinds of behavior to expect when we inadvertently stumble into a particularly nasty mood sequence.

If Ann couldn't find an effective way of dealing with Mike's mood changes, she would have to limit or terminate their relationship before she found herself having to deal with her own perennial destructive mood sequence—the one triggered by the feelings of failure, shame, and humiliation.

CHAPTER 12
EARLY DECISIONS AND DISTORTED PERCEPTIONS

nevitably there comes a time when people get tired of all the theory and the diagnoses and just want to know what to do about the problem that brought them to the office in the first place.

The truth is that relationships are complicated, resistant to change, confusing and, perhaps most importantly, 80 percent of the people who seek out assistance simply want to be heard, not cured. A successful treatment strategy requires awareness, education and the correction of disturbed perceptions that have distorted our view of the world around us. The problem is that most people don't have the time, the energy or the motivation to do what's necessary. Nonetheless, for the 20-30 percent of the people who are willing to do the work, I want to offer this chapter on early decisions, distorted perceptions and the reason we stay in bad marriages even when it's obvious (except to the parties involved) that in extreme cases, the situation may get out of control and possibly be life-threatening.

The Reasons for Acting the Way We Do

Most people who come in for counseling because they feel "crazy" were exposed to ineffectual teaching when they were quite young. Their spouses unwittingly worsen the problems because of their own misguided early decisions as young children. It's not an exaggeration to cite birth as the beginning of what later will become interpersonal problems. We've already noted that "Toxic Personalities" stem from early distortions of their perceptions of "reality." Very generally, problems with attachments begin within the first few months of life; problems with discipline and learning social rules begin around 18 to 36 months. And problems with deciding what we want to get out of life and how we plan to get it begins in the 4- to 7-year range. Of course, faulty learning can be acquired anywhere along the way. Our guides, Ann and Mike, show us how these early decisions played havoc on their relationship.

Soon after discussing mood chains with Mike and Ann, I asked them to describe the results of their first "fight."

Ann recalled thinking, "Here we go again. Every time I think everything will turn out all right, something happens to mess things up."

Mike remembered how discouraged and disheartened he was. He also remembered how he was just as angry with his parents as he was with Ann. When I asked him why, he stated, "I remember wondering how I was going to make things better. Nobody had ever taught me that skill. When my father and my mother fought, my father simply withdrew to the library and read. I guess I still use him as my model, although I know that there's got to be a better way." Without knowing it, Ann and Mike were beginning to address the next topic: Life Scripts.

Life Scripts

Life Scripts reveal the basic decisions people make about their lives and about the paths they have chosen to follow. Couples generally complement each other. The "bully" or domineering person either finds or elicits passivity in his or her partner. The do-gooder often elicits suspicion and distrust.

As we look more deeply into these relationships, we find a reciprocation of attitudes, but also a long, well-defined series of moves and countermoves that reflect the subconscious interpersonal games being played out.

Each of us plays a variety of roles in our interpersonal relationships. We agree, at least at an unconscious level, to obey certain well-established rules. Some of the life scripts we play out are relatively benign; others are destructive and may lead to emotional and/or physical harm to us or to others.

We, all of us, make decisions at a young age in order to secure (1) human contact and stimulation, (2) structure and the comfort of routine, and (3) the establishment of an "existential position" consistent with our self-image and our self-esteem. Taken together, these elements make up a life script, a basic plan defining in concise terms where we want to go in our lives, and how we want to get there. It contains our earliest decisions about ourselves along with our prediction about what "should" happen in the future. Often our life scripts are clear to everyone but us. Some scripts are "bad" because they lead to personal tragedy (alcoholism, depression, psychosis); some are "good" (being a leader, successful husband/wife, handsome prince/ss, effective parent, business wo/man); most fall somewhere in the middle.

A life script is a brief declaration summarizing what we have decided about life and where we are right now, in this moment. The statement usually is felt—even if it is not articulated—in the first person singular. For example, a bad life script might state: "I am drinking myself to death," "I am working myself to death," or, less dramatically, "I am always trying to catch up." A "good" script might declare: "I am rescuing my family (nation)," or "I am bringing harmony to the world."

Whether a life script is benign or harmful depends on our earliest decisions about the nature of our relationship with others (including our relationship with the world, God, mother/father) and our relationship with ourselves. These relationships, boiled down to their very essence, represent four types of existential positions:

Type I: Happy, well-adjusted person. If I believe I'm OK and the world is OK, I will trust and feel accepted. If you (God, Mother/Father, my lover), tell me how smart I am or how pretty I am, I accept what you say, and I feel good about it. I feel happy and optimistic. I can grow up without the need for external support. I maintain well-defined boundaries that help me keep the hostile environment out—including abusive relationships, and help me tolerate uncomfortable feelings inside my skin boundary. I can adjust to adversity, and I can bounce back after failure.

Type II: Unhappy, Neurotic person. If I believe that I'm Not OK but you (the world, God, mother/father, my lover) are OK, I always feel a bit inferior, a bit stupid, or a bit ugly, no matter what you say. But I want you to keep trying to convince me anyway. I am unhappy but not totally miserable. I need support from the outside world, and I become "clingy" and dependent when I don't get it. My boundaries are loose, but I do maintain some control over what comes into my mind and my body, and what I intend to express emotionally and behaviorally. I am not very optimistic about life, and I have trouble adjusting when things get rough, but I manage to muddle through.

Type III: Narcissistic/Paranoid Person. I'm happy knowing I'm always right, and you are always wrong. It doesn't matter if you tell me nice things, because I won't believe you anyway. My job is to exploit you, manipulate you, and take advantage of every situation. If you feel unhappy about my behavior, I will pretend to care, but only until I can figure a way out of the problem. My boundaries are rigid. I won't let anybody know the real me. When my boundaries are breached, I will respond with irritability and possibly with violence. I don't really need you emotionally unless you are willing to confirm my superiority and support my grandiosity.

Type IV: Disorganized/Psychotic Person. I am not happy, and I know deep down you can't be happy either because the world is falling apart. Nobody, including I myself, can be trusted. My boundaries are loose. My thoughts, feelings, and actions can't be contained. The anger, violence, sadness, misery, malevolence, and disorganization around me permeate my boundaries so that I don't clearly understand what is happening to me. Sometimes, to make up for my anxiety and loss of control, I will hallucinate or make up myths (delusions) about my existence. I made up my mind about these things when I was very young—9 to 18 months old—so no one can tell me anything different. Sometimes, however, medication will help me keep my anxiety and my disorganization to a manageable level. I can then function fairly well in society.

These early decisions serve as the bases for any script we choose to write. Depending on our existential position, we predict either a bad future or a relatively happy one. In either case, our early decisions remain with us in one form or another unless—this is the important point—we are able to recognize that our decisions were based on incomplete information, and that we may need to "re-decide" our position. The idea is to replace our malignant perception of the world with a less toxic one.

Once we have made our basic decisions about who we are and what we need, we set out to find someone whose behaviors and attitudes serve as model for us. These models may come from fiction or from real life.

Most often, our parents serve this purpose. However, while our parents often demonstrate how we should play a particular role in our life scripts, they might not be able to show us how to play some of the more important ones. In this case, we choose, either consciously or unconsciously, someone else who can help us actualize our life plan. For example, a Type III (Narcissistic/Paranoid) person may be able to identify with his tyrannical father who teaches the "rules" for behaving in a superior and selfish fashion. However, a mythical character such as Captain Ahab, or a true-to-life character such as Hitler, provides a more dramatic and impressive model. From these characters, we not only learn the basic attitude of the Narcissist/ Paranoid, but also the kinds of goals consistent with a Type III script.

A Type II person who believes she isn't very pretty or bright might well identify with a character in *Cinderella* or, if a male, model himself after the Beast in *Beauty and the Beast*. These models define the beliefs and behaviors that go along with a Type II script.

Whatever our early decisions may be, we need someone to emulate—someone who can teach us what we need to know to satisfy the demands of the life script we have written early in our lives. If our parents do not offer a good model, we will find someone else to do the job.

The Don'ts and the Do's

In addition to our early decisions about the meaning of life and a model to guide us, we are also influenced by the "voices" we have incorporated as part of our personality (review chapter on Passion). Our life scripts are particularly affected by parental injunctions ("Don'ts") and parental attributions ("Do's"). While Dad's words might say, "Idle hands are the devil's handmaidens," his real demand is "Don't be playful" or "Don't be happy." When Mom says, "Big boys/girls don't cry," the message we get—and we believe—is "Don't feel." These kinds of messages reinforce our existential positions and force us to find someone, real or fictional, to show us how we can survive without happiness or without feelings. (Is it any wonder that our children turn to gangs, islands of power in a sea of misery and weakness?)

It is easy to overlook the positive aspects of parental injunctions. After all, they do keep us from stealing and killing, and from coveting our neighbor's wife or husband. In this sense, they are absolutely essential for society. A man whose behavior has not been moderated on occasion can hardly be called civilized, let alone socialized. Nonetheless unreasonable and unnatural demands produce stilted scripts and strained relationships with the significant people in our lives.

Equally damaging are "attributions"—the Do's—of social behavior. "Be brave," "Try harder," "Be a big boy/girl," "Always work hard", etc. are messages most of us received early and often. In themselves, they are good messages. However, when they are unreasonable, they become part of a tragic life script requiring a kind of perfectionism not entirely suited for ordinary humans.

To help us solve the problem of unrealistic attributions we turn again to our mythical heroes: Scarlet O'Hara, Captain Nemo,

Superman, Wonder Woman. Our heroes tell us how to deal with unreasonable but powerful demands, and we include their advice in our life scripts. For example, if the attribution is "Try harder," we might identify with Thomas Edison and become a workaholic; if the attribution is "Be smart," we might identify with Einstein and become a very serious student. We might be very satisfied with our role as a workaholic or serious student. However, when we couple with our lover and have children, our homelife becomes something less than ideal. Our relationship, at all levels, becomes strained and all parties often become thoroughly miserable.

Men and women often share similar scripts. There are members of both sexes who represent happy, neurotic, narcissistic/paranoid, or disorganized/psychotic types. As many men as women have had the "Try harder" message drummed into them, just as there are as many women as men who have had to learn "Don't feel."

As I described the concept of Life Scripts to Ann and Mike, I noted that there were gender differences in the way scripts are advanced and developed. I gave them samples of various scripts and asked them to read them over so that we could discuss the results at our next session. The objective was for each of them (1) to recognize the components of his life script and, more importantly, (2) to appreciate how each one benignly maneuvers the other in order to satisfy his mutual need for human contact, structure, and validation.

Before handing them the samples to be studied, I summarized what we already knew about their scripts.

Ann's script required her to sacrifice herself and her needs for others. It was based on the early teachings of her parents and on her attempt to emulate a mythical heroine. It was not successful because every time she worked out a formula for happiness, she did not include herself in the equation. The resulting disappointment and bitterness nearly drove her mad. She was strong enough, however, to end two destructive relationships and to regain her sense of dignity and pride through a painful process of psychotherapy and a commitment to change.

Mike developed a script requiring him to be logical and rational, to "use his head." Intelligence and education were valued above all else by his parents. He followed the tenets laid down by his father's religious fervor for intellectuality. Had Mike's father remained alive to reinforce his earlier teachings, it is doubtful that Mike would have had the incentive to make badly needed changes. He would have continued to "plan" good relationships, instead of balancing his successful career with the joy of spontaneity and creativity. Ann's affection gave him an opportunity to express his caring and, more importantly, to use his rational mind for altruistic purposes. It gave him an opportunity, in short, to change a possibly tragic script into a more benevolent one.

Women's Scripts

Each life script is based on our early decisions about life, on our parents' injunctions and attributions, and on the people we choose as our models. Below are several fairly typical women's scripts and several of the more common men's scripts.

I suggested to Ann and Mike that as they read the following descriptions, they try to answer the following questions: Who am I, where am I going in my life, and how well do my lover's script and my script fit together? The essence of the exercise is to determine whether they were compatible, not only in their need for Passion/Intimacy/Commitment, but also compatible in terms of their very primary ideas about life and how to live it:

Discounted Child

Margaret is a 36-year-old woman, married to a much older man known for his kindness and generosity. When Margaret was nine years old, she discovered that "growing up" was not allowed. At least, that's what she thinks she learned. Her opinions were never considered. Her parents took her everywhere and showered her with expensive gifts. They anticipated her every need. In turn, Margaret anticipated their need, namely, for her to be incompetent.

She decided at a young age that her parents knew best and felt that to be accepted by them, she had better learn to keep her opinions and feelings to herself. She found they were so protective of her that becoming dependent was the best way to relieve their anxieties. As an adult, she continued to play this role, maintaining a childlike existence, and looking for "parents" to protect her. Fortunately, she found such a person in her older husband.

She soon discovered advantages of the little-girl role. When she complained about the complexities of everyday life, her husband paid special attention to her and shouldered many of the responsibilities that rightfully belonged to her. When she complained of physical ailments, she found she could manipulate her husband into pampering her. Her husband, who, incidentally, went along with the game quite willingly, increased his share of the household chores. In response, Margaret favored him with sex and murmurs of appreciation. Her husband enjoyed the idea of being a hero and found that he was marching double time to the tune Margaret was playing.

After several years, however, he became resentful and disappointed. The feelings just sneaked up on him; he suddenly felt tired and weak, and he imagined the cause of his fatigue was lying in bed next to him. (The real cause, of course, was his own script that required him, like Ann, to give until he literally dropped.)

Nonetheless, Margaret's husband really loved her so he tried to honestly tell her how he felt. Margaret, sensing her security slipping away, fought back by becoming "crazy" both in private and in public. Her husband redoubled his efforts. And he resumed his most successful role—rescuer and "parent" he tolerated the disappointment and the resentment, until finally the strain drained him of too much energy; he became less effective in business and more isolated from his friends.

When he died suddenly of congestive heart failure, people couldn't understand how such a nice man could die so young. Naturally, Margaret was overwhelmed, until, several months after her husband's death, one of his best friends—also older and protective—called Margaret for a date.

When Margaret was little, her favorite character was Cinderella. Now that she had become older, she seems to have carried her early identification with the put-upon future princess into her adult life. She tends to look haggard and overworked although she spends relatively little time working and much time complaining about it. Her new husband frequently notices a worn and piteous expression on her face. He responds—as did his predecessor—with compassion and offers of relief.

Margaret has learned her helpless role well. She spends much of her time listing the many things that make her feel small and unprotected. She becomes overwhelmed by everyday responsibilities. When asked what she could do to remedy the situation, she becomes mute. When pressured to perform arduous but reasonable tasks, she folds up like a house of cards. The people around her take over and do their job plus hers. It is not too long, however, before people begin to realize just how powerful this "Discounted Child" really is.

Margaret's existential position is TYPE II. She fully understands she is weak and inadequate. She hopes those around her really can be counted on to protect her. Her script requires that she validate these perceptions.

In order for Margaret to function as an adult, she needs to decide that there is greater benefit in growing up than in remaining a child. This is a tall order for a woman with her background: she will need to take responsibility for her thoughts, her feelings, and her behavior. She will also need to refuse to seduce people with her helplessness, opting instead to learn more adult ways to handle stress and feelings of inadequacy.

This is dangerous, of course, because if Margaret decides to grow up, her husband cannot play the rescuer role he has embraced. Both parties will then be in foreign territory, playing roles neither one of them understands.

Beauty and the Beast Within

Susan is a beautiful 26-year-old single woman who draws the attention of both men and women. She is pretty enough to be a top model earning an income in six figures. The most eligible bachelors seek her out and, on occasion, some of the most eligible bachelorettes seek her out as well. She discovered early in her teens that people responded only to her face, not her mind. She decided she was never going to be able to earn respect as an ordinary person, so she honed her ability to seduce people with her considerable charm and sensuality.

Behind all the manipulations and seductions, Susan feels angry and resentful about the lack of appreciation and respect. She entertains a stream of both men and women who think they can successfully maneuver her into bed. Unable to express her frustration and resentment directly, she provokes them, promising them excitement and good times, and then fails to deliver the goodies (herself). Occasionally, she does find a Sir Galahad who sweeps her off her feet. Invariably, the encounters are short-lived, Sir Galahad becoming discontented and continuing the search for other damsels in distress.

While Susan feels victimized by Sir Galahad's callousness and deception, she also feels she deserves no better. Despite her facial beauty, she doesn't really feel very good about herself; she doesn't really understand what people see in her. She feels superficial and ugly, and when she looks in the mirror, she sees only her blemishes and none of her true beauty. Compliments are discounted and relegated to the "insincere" pile.

Susan's body is quite beautiful. It is tense and hard, however. She experiences little pleasure from human contact and complains bitterly that men can't turn her on sexually. She hears two voices: one voice tells her she is not worthy as a human being; the other voice tells her no one can be trusted.

She tries to make contact with others—men or women—by provoking them with her stubbornness, sexiness, and dramatics.

When her escorts of either sex respond in kind, Susan becomes outraged. Her escorts become confused and angry, and, more often than not, verbal battles ensue, leaving both Susan and her dates feeling bewildered and disgusted. The odd thing is that while everybody ends up angry, there is also a perverse feeling of stimulation and excitement triggered by the heated exchange of words.

Susan is victimized by a critical voice that refuses to allow her to feel any sense of beauty and dignity. More importantly, there is no way to counteract the effects of the critical voice. Susan's father, a kindly man who could make his daughter giggle and coo, died before Susan could introject—swallow and digest—his words of comfort. The upshot is Susan walks around distrusting everyone; she is sensitive and defensive, and she has earned a reputation for being irritable and grouchy. The voices dominating her life are those of her never-satisfied mother and a frightened, threatened, angry little girl who lost her playfulness and spontaneity when she was merely three years old.

Can't Say No

When Angela was a teenager, she decided she had a weight problem. The real problem is that she had lost control of her physical and psychological boundaries long before her teens. She can't say no to anything. Food, criticism, and compliments filter through her skin boundary as readily as feelings, complaints, and aggression filter out of her skin boundary.

The result is overeating, over-talking, over-drinking, and over-complaining. To maintain her boundaries, she tries diet after diet, hoping that somehow this will prevent her from abusing herself and other people. She tells you she simply wants to feel good about herself, and she wants to gain the acceptance of the people around her.

As a child, she was told to eat everything on her plate. She was not allowed to refuse a second helping at dinner time because, said her mother, "Children all over the world are starving" Angela became obsessed with food as a teenager, and her parents, forgetting how they fostered the weight gain to begin with, sent her to a special camp for overweight girls. In doing so, they sent her a clear message: now she wasn't acceptable even to them!

Angela's inability to say "No" generalized to other aspects of her life. She isn't able to say "No" to anything. Criticism and compliments are devoured as readily as any dessert. She is unable to express anger or resentment, because in a very real sense this too would be like saying "No." She has also discovered that her obesity gives her a certain advantage: She no longer has to deal with the issue of intimacy with men. Ironically, while she feels weak and small inside, her vast bulk makes her feel substantial and solid.

As a young girl, Angela chose Oprah as a model. Whenever the talented talk show host went on a diet, Angela did also. Whenever Oprah changed her hairstyle or her style of dress, Angela saved money until she could buy clothing that matched—in size, if not in quality.

Angela believed her mother's subliminal message to her: "Never refuse anything, good or bad." She also accepted her father's attributions: "Good girls obey their parents." The ultimate result is young woman who acted like a piece of straw bending in the prevailing wind.

Angela needed to develop a benevolent self-image, one allowing her to appreciate herself for what she was. She needed to learn what was good for her, what wasn't, and how to say "No" to unhealthy intrusions (too much food, too much abuse, too much insincere flattery). She needed to appreciate herself for her talents and to understand that, unfortunately, the genetics of obesity play a role she couldn't disregard. She sought counseling to help her rediscover the feelings of intimacy and closeness she lost when she was just a little girl. She joined Overeaters Anonymous to help her recover her lost soul.

Sassy

Lisa, a 34-year-old blonde flight attendant, is single and attractive. She is proud of her self-sufficiency and independence. She established her existential position early in life when she discovered that neither her mother, an alcoholic, nor her father, an overwhelmed man, were available to her and her siblings. She learned at the age of seven it was safer not to depend on others because invariably they let her down.

Asked what she remembers most about her childhood, she will tell you about the great movies she saw on television. She especially enjoyed watching movies that featured "tough" ladies like Bette Davis and Katherine Hepburn. If you press her, she recalls how she and her family were always in the midst of a crisis. Because her mother drank and her father was in and out of the hospital for treatment of depression, Lisa and her brothers and sisters—there were six in all—were told not to reveal anything about the family's affairs. Her mother made it clear it was "us against the world"

Survival depended on learning how to be tough and self-reliant. After years of programming by her mother, Lisa finally figured out she couldn't trust anyone: she decided she have to compete and battle for everything she would ever get. She also learned to suppress feelings of tenderness and any of the emotions that might be mistaken for weakness.

When the Women's Movement gained momentum in the late 1970s, Lisa was one of the first to join. She spent much time being angry at men who, she felt, were weak and ineffectual. She also spent much time being angry at women, who, she felt, were advancing professionally by manipulating weaker males.

Bright and witty, Lisa takes great delight putting down people—men and women alike—for their lack of courage and aggressiveness. Women see her as "castrating"; men see her as "bitchy." Many appreciate her gutsy attitude, but as the years pass, she discovers few people can tolerate her moralistic and irreverent attitude.

Occasionally, she dates men who, at first, seem to enjoy her insightful if somewhat cynical perceptions of the social scene. After several weeks, however, Lisa, feeling seduced and frightened by contact with tender and dependent feelings, puts on the brakes, terminates the relationship, and withdraws until the danger of vulnerability passes.

None of Lisa's dates has ever seen her profound sense of compassion or even suspects that she volunteers at the local hospice comforting terminally ill patients and their families. What they remember most about their experience with her is the vague sense that she simply doesn't trust people, that she goes out of her way to catch people doing something wrong, and then thoroughly enjoys the opportunity of cutting their legs from under them. It seems to them that Lisa's goal is to prove she is better than everybody else.

The upshot of all this are her all too frequent feelings of isolation and bitterness. Suppressed people like Lisa learn that they can count on no one but themselves. They repress the need for hugs, tender words, and harmonious social contact. They are caught up in the "Disgust/Resentment/Vindictive" phase of the Anger and/or Humiliation Emotional Sequence we discussed before. Their salvation lies in re-deciding earlier decisions about trust and about their own omnipotence.

Once mistrust has been supplanted by a sense of goodwill, Lisa will be able to take the normal risks involved in maintaining healthy relationships. The most difficult and necessary part of this process is the need for Lisa to become her own parents, to provide herself with nourishing feelings and warm thoughts of acceptance. The job requires courage and lengthy periods of introspection, often with the aid of a counselor. Lisa will also have to become seriously aware of the family history of alcoholism and depression, both of which put her psychologically and medically at risk.

Men's Scripts

Men also have standard scripts they play out—scripts based on early decisions affecting their later relationships. As we have seen, Mike's life script could have had a tragic effect on his relationship with Ann. Fortunately, he had discovered his script needed to be modified. He was also bright enough, courageous enough, and energetic enough to make the necessary changes. Mike's script prioritized the need for logic and the rational mind. While these traits per se were not destructive, the lack of balance was. Mike, with much help from various healing experiences—visits to Ashrams, Esalen, Tibetan Holy Men, and Ann's love—was able to learn how to balance logic with compassion.

There are many other scripts men write for themselves. Several of the most common are described below.

Imposter

Howard is an impostor. He decided early on that he was small and inadequate. His lack of self-esteem required that he (and everyone else in the world) see him as the commander-and-chief, decision-maker, wheeler-dealer, and head honcho in his relationships. In reality, he is less bright and capable than his wife of eight years, and he makes considerably less money. His modest success in business is due in large part to her industriousness and creativity. He organizes the business and arranges the social calendar; he pays the bills and keeps the books. Howard knows—or at least senses—he is less competent than her, but he suppresses this feeling. With this vague awareness come the twin emotions of guilt and resentment.

He accepts his wife's judgments, but he makes it perfectly clear he is still the boss. Invitations to friends, telephone book listings, and letters to relatives include both his and his wife's names, but invariably his name is listed first. Howard doesn't feel good about being a phony, about usurping the credit that rightfully belongs to his wife. However, he feels even less good about not living up to the sexist credo advanced by his father (and accepted by his mother!): marriage is an equal partnership with the wife just slightly less equal than the husband.

To maintain harmony and a sense of balance in his relationship, Howard needs to understand the concept of authenticity.

Authenticity is made up of equal parts of acceptance of self and acceptance of others. If the pendulum swings too far in either direction for a prolonged period of time, self-esteem will suffer and the relationship will suffer along with it. The essential treatment for Howard is to become authentic in his support for his more able wife—to appreciate the need for a balance of acceptance in the marriage. In short, Howard's level of Intimacy needs to be increased. Feelings of phoniness, guilt and resentment simply evaporate when intimacy replaces submerged but deeply felt feelings of incompetence.

Hot Stuff

Hot Stuff is best represented by Dennis, a 34-year-old divorced father of three. He readily admits that emotionally he is still an 18-year-old, but he doesn't really believe it. Everybody else does.

Dennis spends his entire adult life chasing after, with varying degrees of success, "Movie Stars" and "Beauty and the Beast Within." He is searching, he will tell you, for the perfect woman. He readily believes the media hype about perfect 10s. On any given day, he is found at the magazine rack in the local bookstore, checking out the latest issues of *Playboy* and *Gentlemen's Quarterly*.

Dennis decided at an early age that Broadway Joe Namath (former New York Jets quarterback) was one of the few real men around, and he has been trying to emulate him ever since.

Dennis' mother was a hard-working, totally caring woman who, of her three children, selected Dennis as "special." She never said "No" to him, readily gave in to his wishes, and protected him from adversity. So deeply did she feel for him, she (and the other children) went without essentials to provide him with the best clothing and the not-always-affordable little sports car he wanted. Dennis' father didn't always agree with his wife, but he felt he couldn't go against her wishes without arousing her ire. Dennis, as we can see, was "spoiled." His feelings and judgments were never questioned. Eventually, without the appropriate reality checks offered by mature parents, he came to believe the fantasies offered by magazines and television were what life was really about.

Dennis learned from his experiences as a youngster that, "you should never settle for second best." He defined "second-best" as anybody with whom he didn't want to be seen. These included "ugly" women and those who were "too straight." It wasn't that he didn't like these women; he simply felt they didn't fit in with his little-red-sports-car lifestyle.

For the most part, Dennis was attracted to the "Movie Star" and the "Beauty and the Beast Within" types. His relationships with both kinds of women were disastrous. While they were often terrific companions in public—after all, they did dress well and that did attract the jealous attention of both men and women—there seemed to be something missing in the relationship. "Movie Stars" could contribute nothing to a conversation other than gossipy appraisals of various entertainers. "Beauty and the Beast Within" types proved to be too bright, too perceptive, and too explosive, not at all the kind of unconditional adoration Dennis wanted.

Both kinds of women initially enjoyed Dennis' attention. The Movie Star liked the way he showed her off to his friends; Beauty and the Beast Within thoroughly enjoyed seducing him, manipulating him into making promises both knew he couldn't keep and then lowering the boom when he didn't. The mutually satisfying seduction phase of these relationships invariably wore thin after the first few dates. Dennis couldn't deliver the glamour and excitement he promised, and his dates became sulky and resentful.

Given the brevity of these relationships, it would appear that these life scripts are incompatible. In truth, they are not: Hot Stuff finds these women and they make themselves found, because all parties involved need an excuse to avoid intimacy. "Incompatible" life scripts serve this purpose admirably. While all parties appear to be resentful, angry, hurt, etc., the termination of each relationship actually brings relief to all the people involved. Hot Stuff is saved once again from giving up his most precious possession: his ego. Movie Star is saved from having to recognize that she really isn't a Movie Star. And Beauty and the Beast Within is saved from the pain of having to risk yet another abandonment.

The end result is that Dennis rededicates himself to the search for the perfection. He works hard to make a lot of money with which to buy the attentions of other women. The women most likely to respond to his flattery and lifestyle are—you guessed it—MS and BBW. If Dennis is bright enough, and if he hasn't been too spoiled by the uncritical and unrealistic devotion of his mother, time and (s)experience will teach him there are not too many "10s" in the real world, no matter how many times his parents communicated messages to the contrary. He will begin to appreciate the humanity in all women, and he will learn how to combat his fear of invasion, i.e., intimacy. He will also begin to appreciate the nature of his life script, and he will find a woman who cannot only tolerate but actually enjoy his childlike qualities—his sexiness and his need for attention—while at the same time nudge him closer to edges of intimacy.

Chesty

William (his parents call him Billy) is a handsome 24-year-old man who decided at the age of 14 that maleness and athletic accomplishment were one and the same. He took a Charles Atlas muscle-builder course, lifted weights with his friends and tried out successfully for varsity sports. He prided himself on being one of the few lettermen in school.

Five days a week, you could find him on the basketball court practicing with a semi-pro team. Every morning, before work, you found him in the gym, building and rebuilding his body, defining his muscles, looking spiffy in his black spandex trunks. It seems that he would rather be in the gym than be with a girl, an irony since one of the reasons he gives for working out so often is that he wants to make himself more attractive.

As Billy got older, he discovered that most women responded better to gentle words than to hardened muscle. Since he had no gentle words—or gentle thoughts for that matter—he began to feel isolated and unappreciated. Overwhelmed by isolation, exacerbated by the fact that most of his friends were married, he began to drink large quantities of alcohol and to eat even larger quantities of food. At home (he still lived with Mom and Dad), he spent many hours watching sporting events on television, reminiscing with his father about "the good old days" when he was able to run the hundred-yard dash in 9.4 seconds. His dates—the few he had—often complained that he couldn't talk about current events or anything not related to macho things.

Billy's father always emphasized the competitive aspects of any encounter. There always had to be a winner, he would tell Billy, often while the two were working on a fifth of Bourbon during half-time. They enjoyed putting "egg heads" down, because "they had no common sense" even if they could make money.

Billy accepted these attributions as real, never questioning his father's observations. It wasn't until Bill Bradley, a basketball star who later became a politician, extolled the virtues of intelligence that Billy became even dimly aware that his interest in athletics was not antithetical to reading a book from the *New York Times* best seller's list. When he told his father he had decided to take night courses at the local college, Dad was not impressed. Fortunately, his mother was; she encouraged him through words and careful attention to continue to build his mind with the same vigor with which he built his body. Billy stuck with it until he earned an Associates Degree. He also stuck with a diet of good food. Finally, he joined Alcoholics Anonymous. This left his father sitting alone in front of the television on many a night. Billy felt a bit guilty about this, but his guilt abated once he met a woman who appreciated Billy's efforts and who enjoyed teaching him the gentleness he never seemed to pick up from his parents.

Never Trust a Woman

Jim is a 38-year-old career soldier. His father, a retired Master Sergeant in the Marine Corps, is his idol. They spent much time together when Jim was young, Father always reminding his son that men and women were different. The main difference, he said, is "You can never trust a woman." Father also implied you could never trust anyone else either, but women, in his view, were particularly evil.

Jim observed his parents closely after this revelation, and in a period of years, he discovered that his father really didn't trust women, especially Jim's mother. But he couldn't understand why: she gave everything she had to her children—Jim, his brother and his two sisters. She cleaned and cooked, and washed their clothes. She read bedtime stories to them and bandaged their cuts and scrapes.

No matter: Jim believed his father. He did not discern the Master Sergeant's basic paranoid posture (Type III existential position).

Jim's favorite movie was *Patton* with George C. Scott in the lead role. He learned from Patton that ruthlessness, obstinacy, pride, glory and courage in the face of danger were the most important ingredients in any man's life. Jim joined the service immediately after graduating from high school. He remained a bachelor, spending most of his available time in the pursuit of all-male activities. For sexual release, Jim was quite comfortable visiting a brothel near the base where he was stationed.

As Jim became older, he became increasingly bitter. His friends, he felt, had abandoned him by getting married and settling into decidedly unmale roles of obedient husbands and fathers. At family affairs, he felt out of place and different.

His bitterness grew. He felt alone and empty. Neither his father nor Patton had prepared him for this!

He discovered through these experiences his father was correct: he could trust neither men nor women. Once, however, he did find a woman he wanted to marry. But shortly before the wedding date, the injunctions Jim learned about intimacy, passion, and commitment took control and he backed out of the marriage, leaving a hurt and perplexed almost-bride-to-be trying to figure out what had gone wrong.

Fear of deception and betrayal compromised Jim's judgment. As his suspicions grew, so did his penchant for building a case against people, not just women but men as well. Nurturant behavior on the part of others, that is, loss of control, was simply unacceptable from anyone.

Jim now spends a substantial portion of his monthly allotments at the local tavern. Precisely after his third drink, he finds someone who will listen while he lists all the things that went wrong in his life because of women. Of course, all the other Jims at the bar listen attentively, joining in the chorus with stories of their own.

Unfortunately, "curing" Jim of these attitudes is extremely difficult. The toxicity of his father's injunctions against intimacy prevents Jim from trusting anyone enough to help him balance his view of the world. More than likely, Jim will end up doing exactly what he is doing now—drinking at the local bar and wondering how much better off he would be "if it weren't for women." On occasion, his father, Jim's idol, now a disgruntled old man—somehow even older since the premature death of his wife—joins Jim at the bar and talks about his lovely wife who abandoned him in death when he needed her the most.

Before we get to the "Treatment "part of this chapter, let's see what Ann and Mike say.

Life Script Exercises for Ann and Mike

To help Ann and Mike understand the importance of life scripts, I asked them to go back to the earliest memories they had of their parents, caretakers, or other powerful adults in their lives. The "best" memories, for the purposes of this exercise, were the ones representing events occurring prior to the age of four. After each had sifted through half a dozen memories or so, I asked each to summarize in his mind what he believed to be his essential belief about himself and about the world. For example, let's say that the earliest memories include: (1) being punished for getting dirty, (2) witnessing the behavior of an alcoholic parent, (3) being embarrassed by a nursery school teacher, and (4) not being able to run as quickly as other children. The cumulative impact of these memories might have led to the belief, "I'm small and weak; everyone is stronger, smarter, and prettier than I am." I told Ann and Mike, "Describe your early decision about yourself, your relationship with the world, and your "existential position."

Ann's response: "I remember being carried home by my mother from a friend's house. It was very late and I was tired. She was tired too, but she picked me up and carried me, and I'll never forget how that made me feel."

My response: "How did it make you feel?"

Ann's response: "It made me feel small but protected. It also made me feel spoiled, like maybe I would never have to worry about anybody not being there if I really needed them." (Ann became sad, and her eyes moistened for a moment.)

"Do you see any relationship between that decision and your relationship with men?"

Ann's response: "Unfortunately, it's all too clear. I always expect to be 'carried' and I always find someone who is strong enough to 'carry' me both financially and emotionally. I wonder if I'll ever outgrow that feeling. I'm like one of those Type II neurotics who seems to be so dependent on everyone. Come to think of it, even though she worked hard, I always felt close to that maid in the movie, *Gone with the Wind*. My script seems to be 'Depending on you.'"

Ann began to cry in earnest at that point. Mike put his arm around her shoulder and gave her the hug she seemed to need.

It was Mike's turn. I said, "Have you been able to come up with an early memory that summarizes your view of the world?"

Mike seemed to be reluctant to speak. I urged him on.

"I remember a time when I drowned four little kittens."

Ann and I both looked at him. Mike looked down, ashamed, saddened, perhaps even terrified by his admission. I didn't need to say anything.

"I must have been three or four years old. Our cat had delivered a litter of beautiful kittens in the closet in our living room. It had happened before—unwanted kittens— and the solution to the problem seemed to be to get rid of them by placing them in a paper bag and simply throwing them into the river. It was common practice where we lived. The older children in the neighborhood seemed to think nothing of it. I had no idea of the meaning or the value of life or death. I thought that was simply the way it's done. I wanted to be like everyone else, so I threw the poor kittens into the river, thinking perhaps that somehow, they would float down to a field or somewhere where they would be safe. I wonder now if my position on abortion has something to do with that simple gesture—the murder of four little kittens."

The confession was overwhelming. Mike had rediscovered a memory that he had long ago buried—a memory that revealed his need to be accepted by everyone else.

Mike continued: "With regard to my existential position—that's a hard one. I had thought that I was one of your Type I "Happy" people. Now I'm not so sure. Maybe I'm just a Type II neurotic who needs a lot of loving. My script is 'Following orders' or maybe 'Needing to be accepted.'" Another admission, another step forwards.

We then discussed models who served to help implement the early script decisions. Ann's model turned out to be comedienne Gracie Allen, a supposed ditzy woman fully dependent on her husband (comedian George Burns) and extremely funny. "I always liked Gracie Allen," Ann said, "because she was able to be dependent without being self-conscious or embarrassed by it."

Mike's model was his father, who, despite his emotional coolness, was able to show Mike how to be aloof and yet who somehow managed to get the attention he needed from his wife and co-workers. His mother had taught him that in order to be socially and professionally accepted, Mike had to learn how to be charming. His father taught him that humor and intelligence were the two ways to accomplish these goals, although he—Mike's father—seemed to have relatively little of the former and an overabundance of the latter.

We next talked about attributions and injunctions. Ann recalled that her mother always emphasized the virtue of self-sacrifice and the need to "hold your tongue" no matter how angry you were. The reason was, she told Ann, that patience and the suppression of anger were not only signs of maturity, but also signs of "class," an attribute that "makes all the difference in the world" when it came time to attract the "right kind of man."

Mike's parents emphasized the need to "be logical" and to be "responsible." His father was fond of saying, "Don't be silly" despite the fact that, after a few drinks, he himself could become uproariously whimsical and witty. The result was Mike's very serious and business-like appreciation of humor. Fortunately, Ann was able to reduce the seriousness and increase the humor in a more balanced way.

Both Ann and Mike agreed that the only cure for them was to be together forever. Who was I to argue?

So, one answer to the "treatment" of destructive life scripts is to develop a relationship with a healthy person, and, while you are waiting for that to happen, establish relationships with people who can fill in the gaps of your experience. Find people whose view of the world is less cynical than yours, people who can give you a second-chance family where you can learn the skills and the perceptions you need in order to survive in an often-challenging social environment. Decide to join a group that can respect your goodness and appreciate your value as a sentient being. Become aware of your perceptions and decide that you will be open to the views of others, others who you can trust, who can demonstrate more acceptable and more effective ways of dealing with everyday issues at home, at work, and at play.

Am I suggesting a therapy group of some kind? That is one strategy to be sure. Depending on the type of "therapy" the group leader advocates, some groups are incredibly effective. But in many situations, AA, or a local book club, or silent retreats in the ashrams of Colorado or India, or an experience in living in a kibbutz in Israel may be perfect vehicles for delivering the kinds of life lessons that we have been talking about.

Am I suggesting individual "therapy"? Probably not. I believe that a group of people who can offer a second-chance family situation will be far more helpful.

What about a psychiatrist who could prescribe medication?

That's a fine idea if you have problems that are chemically based. But be mindful that usually we need models who can show us the "path with a heart." Medications can do a lot and they play a role in our idea of a curative program but the hard work of learning about Intimacy, Passion, and Commitment still lies ahead.

CHAPTER 13

TRUTH AND THE REPAIR OF A BROKEN RELATIONSHIP

<hr>

Ann and Mike had already tested the viability of their relationship. Despite their concerns about Mike's readiness for commitment, they decided to keep plugging along. Each offered the other enough passion, intimacy, and commitment to evoke good feelings about himself and about the world. Had they decided that there was no realistic chance of resolving differences in lifestyle, values, motivation, emotional climates, or in life scripts, they would have had to remove themselves from the situation, a heart-rending decision.

The process of parting is more difficult than the process of coupling. During the process of coupling, the contact and connection phases often are based on differences, and differences produce excitement. Excitement becomes its own reward and reinforces romantic notions. As a relationship develops, couples work hard to find points of agreement and to develop a sense of sameness. Each person learns to adapt to his lover's view of the world, and to accept his flaws and eccentricities. In short, each member of the couple learns to balance the seesaw, balancing the differences with the sameness that led to stability and to security.

To quit the relationship now, you would have to abandon your lover—an arduous task after so many months, perhaps years—of emotional investment. You would also have to retool your emotions for yet another sortie into yet another contact-connection-coupling Tilt-A-Whirl with yet another potential candidate for your affections.

Splitting up requires stamina and a not-easily-described quality of character called "courage." Courage is the most important of all the tools for changing various aspects of our lives. Without it, no change can be made; with it, almost any change is possible.

Courage in relationships transcends logic and reason; it comes from a process much more profound than simply "figuring things out." It comes from the ultimate "moment of truth," the precise moment when, upon laying your head on the pillow before a fitful sleep, you are able to clearly say, "This isn't going to work." And then you take action, recognizing you are about to enter an emotional marathon requiring time, patience, and resilience.

The completion of the exercises at the end of each of the previous chapters gave Ann and Mike some insight into their courtship. I would hope that they have also given you some insight about you and your lover. You may have already decided whether your relationship will live or die, or, more likely, whether a vague sense of indecision prevails.

The experiments presented later in this chapter will clarify the nature of your discontent. They will magnify strengths and weaknesses. If completed conscientiously, the experiments will improve your understanding of what is wrong—of what gives you the feeling of Not-OKness. Or, conversely, you will develop a better understanding of why the current relationship is so important that you want to expand it, and spend the rest of your life with your lover.

The Secret of Change

The paradoxical secret of changing yourself or your situation is often to do nothing. Deliberate attempts to change will frequently fail. Your mind and your emotions resist change the same way the infant resists an unpalatable dose of strained spinach.

The resistance is expressed through the voice of the recalcitrant child in all of us—the part of us that says, "You can't push me around!" in response to a critical parent voice that demands that we "do better" next time.

With the resistance come fragmented feelings and thoughts. A part of us wants to change, our inner child's voice saying, "I need to change because Mother/Father will abandon me if I don't." But there is another part—just as strong—that doesn't want to change. This voice declares, "I'm an adult and I don't need you to tell me what to do!"

The battle between these two parts leaves us exhausted and drained, and the coercive attempt to change results in conflict, confusion, and uncertainty. These feelings make our efforts to change hardly worth the time and the effort. At best, our changes will be temporary. At worst, we impede, distort, and disguise our real needs and, along with them, the true nature of our relationship with our lover.

The question is: if we can't deliberately change our situation, or us, how will change occur? The answer is: an awareness of who we are, and what we need to sustain our feeling of humaness.

Changes in our awareness lead automatically to other changes in our lives. For example, to develop self-esteem and a more benevolent self-image, we need to increase an awareness of our skills, our talents, and our essential goodness. To develop a joy of life and spontaneity, we need to increase our awareness of the now moment, and we need to learn to let go of the past.

The trick is to appreciate our own experience of the world, to let us flow with our feelings and thoughts, without resisting momentary discomfort. Change born of awareness brings with it an intuitive recognition of what is healthy and alive for us in the present, in the now.

The Nature of Awareness

Awareness is not easily understood in the abstract because, as soon as we become aware of an experience, we lose it. Awareness refers to a life process that cannot be divided into its parts. It is an ever-changing experience of how we (inside the skin boundary) respond to the world around us (outside the skin boundary), and how we bridge the two worlds through picture-thoughts. The awareness of our internal world and our external world changes continuously; we can never experience it exactly the same way twice. Just as we cannot take a handful of river water and say, "This is the river," we cannot take a handful of awareness—take a Polaroid picture of an ongoing experience—and say, "This is reality."

Awareness requires perceiving ourselves within the context of our life space. Our life space includes all the elements influencing our behavior at any given time. These may include personal influences, environmental influences, or the more elusive influences of politics, economics, and institutions (media, education, societal decrees, religion, or philosophy).

Becoming aware means the simultaneous perception of three spheres: (1) our internal sensations and feelings, (2) our experiences of external "real" things, and (3) our world of picture-thoughts. It is a full-time job. People who want to succeed in their relationships accept the challenge of the task eagerly. They want to know about themselves, and about the world out there. They want to know how much they can grow spiritually and emotionally; they want to expand their boundaries to include the not-me experiences. They want to enjoy a good laugh, and to create opportunities to experience the act of being alive. And they want most of all to contribute to the beauty and dignity of their lover.

There is only a handful of truly aware people. We can recognize them easily: they are spontaneous, curious, competent, perceptive, sensitive, optimistic, cooperative, and sharing. They move around with a certain grace and aplomb. Their boundaries are loose enough to welcome us in, and yet not too loose. They are aware of their environment—internal and external—in ways that most of us will never experience.

Awareness is critical to compatibility with our lover, compatibility with our own needs, fears and desires, and compatibility with our ever-evolving life circumstances. This compatibility mirrors our appreciation of the three spheres of awareness.

Outer-World Awareness

There are three spheres of awareness. The first is awareness of the outside world. This refers to our ability to make full contact with everything on the other side of the contact boundary. These include things like smells, tastes, sounds, tangibles, and sights—everything we experience out there at the present moment.

It is made up of people, places, jobs, family, hobbies, the highest mountains, the reddest sunsets, the bluest skies, and the whitest snows. It also contains the best books and the most delicious meals. In short, it is the place where we make contact with the experiences that move us to tears, laughter, and anger, where we earn our wages, and where we strain our muscles. And it is the place where we exchange our potential for the good life for the reality of joy.

Stimulation from the outer world is so important that, fully deprived of it for even a few hours, we become "psychotic" in the sense that we begin to hallucinate in an attempt to fill the void. For example, there has been research indicating that over 60 percent of the spouses who survive the death of their mates after long marriages experience auditory and/or visual hallucinations connected with their deceased partners.

If we cannot directly experience the other side of what each of us calls "me," we will simulate the environment through fantasies so powerful, they may become our reality. In short, outer-world stimulation must be established, if we are to maintain a palatable life. Is it any wonder that adults locked in solitary confinement or in states of emotional withdrawal (or children locked in closets) behave in such odd ways?

Inner-World Awareness

Our bodies are made up of bones, skin, muscles, and tissues. They represent both the foundation and the protective shelter for our physical being. They also represent the seat of our sensations and emotions, the domains making up the world on this side of our skin-boundary. The integrity of bodily functions depends on our diligence in repairing the body when it breaks down, and on reinforcing its strength with food, vitamins, and exercise. Excesses of any kind serve to destroy the body's integrity as surely as wind, rain, and corrosion conspire to weaken our strongest homes and buildings. Lungs filled with smoke, brain cells battered by alcohol, muscles compromised by junk foods, and hearts hardened by cholesterol often leave in their wake tragic illness and death.

The unprotected and weakened body is vulnerable to physical dis-ease and to emotional dis-ease as well. Bad thoughts and bad feelings, grouchiness and irritability, depression, and cynicism are signs that we have begun to take our bodies for granted. Unlike old cars, we cannot trade in our physical selves every two years no matter how dysfunctional they become.

In the inner world—the world on this side of the contact boundary—we experience sharp contacts with sensations such as itching, tension, and warmth, and with feelings such as anger, happiness, contentment, and sadness. We own these experiences; we understand them to belong to us, and we take full responsibility for them.

Outer-world and inner-world awareness have one thing in common: reality. Itching and palpitations of the heart are as real as the smell of a rose or the feel of silk. While the inner world is subjective—a world no one else can experience—the outer world is objective and verifiable. The two worlds taken together make up what most people call real world.

Middle-World (Fantasy) Awareness

The third zone of interest to us occupies the smallest space, but also contains the greatest potential for comfort and success in our personal relationships. This is the place where imagination and thinking supplement sensing and experiencing. It is our mental and spiritual zone. It reflects precisely how our bodies and the environment meet, and how we negotiate the process of living. The interaction between the body and the environment creates the thing we call mind, the exact whereabouts of which is unknown, and will always be unknown. Some people would suggest that in actuality it is an internalized image of our godliness or our soul. I wouldn't disagree.

This third sphere of awareness is especially important when we talk about relationships because it comprises fantasies that have no verifiable basis in reality. Fantasy includes experiences such as imagining, thinking, planning, guessing, stage fright, and memories. The experiences cannot be measured per se; we can, however, measure the effect our fantasies have on our behavior. Tightened jaws, knotted stomachs, panic attacks, feelings of betrayal, "paranoid" thoughts, and infatuation are just several of the many ways we know that fantasy is exerting its influence on us and, inevitably, on our relationships.

While the process of fantasizing takes place in the present, the content of fantasy is timeless. Our imaginings, thoughts, and planning pay no heed to reality. Neither inner strivings nor outer pressures restrict us; our fantasies take on a life of their own without regard to bodily sensations or societal demands. We can fantasize about the past or the future; we can hallucinate the smell of the rose, or a frightening vision of bugs crawling over our bodies. Whatever the content of our fantasies, we do not make full contact with the inner/outer world experience, and we, therefore, have abandoned a sacred event at the contact boundary.

Fantasy is extremely important to us. Within each imagining, each picture, each guess, there is a truth—a germ of some hidden reality that teaches us something about us, and about our immediate relationship with our lover/partner.

Exercises in Awareness

I introduced a series of graded awareness exercises to Ann and Mike in this way:

"To derive full benefit from the following exercises, allow yourself to contact all three spheres of awareness—the outer world, the inner, and the fantasy, or middle, world. Do not be alarmed or disappointed if you become confused, uncomfortable, anxious, or self-conscious. Each exercise is designed to bring a certain kind of awareness that will help you understand the essence of your relationship with yourself and with your lover. After you sift through your experiences, you will become better at communicating the maximum truth with a minimum of discomfort. Please remember this: growth takes time. Don't be impatient; don't try to change. Repeat the exercises as often as you need until you have gleaned a "truth" from your efforts."

Exercises: Three Spheres

I wanted to clarify the concept of awareness, so I told Ann and Mike to try the following nine exercises: the first experiment appears to be quite simple. It is, however, extraordinarily difficult for most people. Since it forms the foundation for all future exercises, spend as much time as you need to complete it.

Sit in a comfortable position. Become aware of all three zones. Become aware of one inner-world experience (for example, heartbeat, breathing, sensations). Then become aware of one outer-world experience (for example, the warmth of the room, feet touching the floor), and then one fantasy-world experience (for example, wondering whether you are doing the exercise correctly, or planning for the dinner party Saturday night). Become an observer of your awareness.

Tell yourself what your awareness is: "Here and now I am aware of (tension in my neck, music on the stereo, imagining what my lover is doing, etc.). Repeat the cycle five times; that is, five internal awareness', five external awareness', and five fantasy awareness', always in the same order. Notice where your awareness wanders. Do you feel more comfortable becoming aware of inner or with outer-world experiences? Are you able to follow a fantasy to its "logical" conclusion, or is your train of thought disrupted by competing fantasies?

Appreciate the difference between fantasy and reality. Notice that when you focus on fantasy, inner/outer experiences disappear and vice versa. Notice how you describe your experiences. Do you use verbs (e.g., the picture makes me happy), sensations (e.g., my arm is tensing up) or feeling words (e.g., this exercise makes me nervous)? Do you find yourself remembering events from the past, or perhaps wondering about things in the future? Stay with the process of experiencing your world. How long can you concentrate before you are distracted by a thought or a picture?

After you have trained yourself to become aware of the three zones, conjure up a picture of your lover. Follow the image of your lover as it changes. (Remember when you were a kid and you watched clouds form and reform into various shapes or images?) Become aware of the effect your lover's image/actions have on you. Do you begin to experience tension, excitement, or anger? Do you perhaps begin to want to fantasize about what s/he is doing at this moment, or about what will happen in the future? Get in touch with the quality of the experiences. What is the message—the truth—behind the pictures? Use an "I" statement to summarize the message: for example, "I get so mad when I think about how s/he treats me" or "I really miss him/her."

Exercise 2: Identifying with Perceptions

Let your attention wander until something "grabs" it. Focus on the object. Appreciate its structure: is it round, square, or a combination of shapes? Is it heavy, light, or weightless? Imagine what it would be like if you were the object. What would you experience? For example: if your attention rests on a lamp, what would you experience if you were a lamp? ("I am a lamp. I am bright. I am useful because I enable others to see when it's dark outside, etc.") After you identify with the object for several minutes, discover what you and the object really have in common. Perhaps you really are bright, and you really do enlighten people with your wisdom or intelligence. What truth can you learn about yourself that you may have forgotten or never truly appreciated before? Spend about five minutes on this exercise. If you have difficulty with it the first time, try it again.

Once you have gleaned a truth about yourself, imagine that you tell your lover about it. What is his/her reaction to it? Does s/he appreciate your skills, talents, or potential?

Exercise 3—Boundary Skipping

Having introduced Ann and Mike to the idea of exercises, I then asked them to engage in a series of personal experiments designed to test the underpinnings of their relationship. It was important for them to confront each other directly about their experiences and to truthfully discuss their feelings. The results led to the first shreds of discord, but it was short-lived—much to the relief of both people.

I told them: "By now, you realize that the contact boundary marks the place where the environment and the thing called 'I' meet. It's the place where we accommodate the world around us. There would be no laughter, no breathing, no creativity without the I/environment contact. There are times, however, when withdrawal from the environment serves a very good purpose. The following exercise offers an opportunity to learn more about the contact/withdrawal process.

Begin by experiencing as completely as possible your external world, for example, the temperature in the room, the chair you're sitting on, the clothes you are wearing, the sounds surrounding you, etc. Is it pleasant, unpleasant, or neutral?

When you have a sense of the external world, close your eyes and let yourself withdraw. Give yourself permission to let your mind wander anywhere it would like to go.

Experience what it is like to deliberately leave your environment. Where does your imagination lead you? A place inside the skin-boundary? Outside? To a more exciting, more rejuvenating, more relaxing, more colorful, more populated place?

Now come back to the here and now of your environment. How do you experience the transition? Would you rather be in the outer zone of your environment or in the fantasyland you just left?

Now close your eyes once again and allow your mind to wander. Do you go back to the same place as before? Open your eyes and compare the experiences. What is it like in here compared to out there?"

Ann responded first. "I like being 'out there.' I think that's why I became a writer in the first place. I could go anywhere and do anything I wanted to do. I could be with anyone I wanted to be with, and if I didn't like something, I could change it. I become energized when I'm in my fantasy world, and while I realize I need come back to reality every once in a while, I find most daily chores pure drudgery."

Mike admitted to occasional lapses in his preference for more realistic activities, but generally he enjoyed the competitive world. "My energy," he said, "comes not from battling fictions and monsters. I enjoy the competition of real people in real time."

"How does this affect your relationship with Ann?" I asked.

"Why, it makes it sexier and more exciting!"

"Sexier and more exciting?" I was confused.

"Why, of course! Ann's wonderful imagination and her fantasy world completely complement my need for real-time structure. She imagines it, and I make it happen! It works out perfectly. She fantasizes and writes about it; I read it and bring it to reality."

I only needed to look at Ann's smiling face to know that the two really had learned how to make their differences work for them.

Withdrawal into fantasy serves us best when it allows us to escape difficult or painful realities. Under extreme stress, we can withdraw back to a time and a place when we felt better and behaved better. With luck, when we return to the real, more-difficult situation, we can bring back with us the excitement and the power that we find in the withdrawn state. The additional energy we find in our fantasyland helps us cope with a less-than-comfortable reality.

Clearly, too much withdrawal leads to isolation, a state of mind that, by its very nature, precludes the kind of human contact necessary to relieve loneliness. It is likewise clear that prolonged withdrawal from very difficult situations will only exacerbate the difficulties. The choice, then, appears to be to either hold onto unpleasant realities, or to make full contact with the pressure-relieving fantasy which has, as its by-product, a disruption of the process of dealing with our problems.

The other option is to make contact with the unpleasant, disturbing reality until we feel marginally uncomfortable, and then to withdraw into our inner world until we can rejuvenate ourselves, and then to prepare ourselves for the next skirmish with adversity.

All three zones of awareness are useful and necessary, but preoccupation with any specific zone brings a host of problems. For example, too much fantasy activity, because it disrupts full contact with the real world, may prevent us from dealing effectively with everyday issues. The lack of balance produces a loss of awareness and diminishes our ability to function optimally.

When we feel threatened, our hearts beat faster, our blood pressure increases, and our muscles tense up to prepare us for battle or for retreat. If, however, we only imagine a threat, our rapid heart rate and the accompanying preparations for fight or flights sap us of our energy, and we find even the simplest tasks burdensome. Another example: if we have "stage fright" and imagine others will judge our performance harshly, we experience the discomfort of "self-consciousness." Our fantasy, generally a catastrophic expectation, makes us want to remove ourselves from the threatening situation. Here we are, center stage: we want to run, and yet we are compelled to remain on stage. The result is a battle between the part of us that wants to withdraw (to inhibit behavior) and the part that wants to run (to exhibit behavior). With so much energy devoted to keeping control, there is little energy left over to do our act (asking for a date, making a toast, making a speech, etc.).

On the other hand, too little involvement in fantasy will also drain us of our energy. A constant barrage of immutable stress—poverty, illness, loss of a lover, arguments at home—may lead to a variety of physical and emotional illnesses, as well as just plain misery. Fantasy provides us with a reservoir of hope and excitement. The irony is that too much fantasy leads to conflict, confusion, and dis-integration; too much harsh reality leads to the same set of disruptive behaviors!

As the last step in this exercise, I asked Ann and Mike to remember their most recent intimate contact. I suggested that they get a sense of what it was like to be with each other in a particular setting, doing a particular thing. I then suggested that they withdraw into their by-this-time-familiar fantasyland, bringing their images of intimacy with them. I asked them to compare the two experiences. Was the remembered real situation more satisfying and comfortable? Or, rather, did the fantasy feel more secure and exciting? Ann and Mike each completed this sentence:

Compared to my real lover, my fantasy lover is

Ann's response: "Compared to my real lover, my fantasized lover is tame and somewhat inept!"

Mike's response: "Compared to my real lover, my fantasy lover could learn a few things!"

Clearly, Ann and Mike enjoyed each other in real life, and, while they readily admitted to having wonderful imaginings about each other, nothing could compare to their being with one another in an embrace of intimacy. I was beginning to wonder why they had sought counseling in the first place.

Exercise 4—"Create-A-Product"

The "Create-A-Product" exercise is one of the best tools for learning about how people see themselves in relation to other people.

"Self-image" is perhaps the single most important determinant of success or failure in any given relationship. It comprises the totality of pictures, thoughts, and feelings we have about us. How we see us today will determine to a very large degree how we will behave, think, and feel tomorrow.

I asked Ann and Mike to begin the exercise with this simple task:

"Think of a product you feel society needs or values. The product can be anything. Be creative. Let your mind be silly or serious. For example, golfers may be interested in an automatic ball chaser. A psychotherapist may be interested in inventing an inflatable grandmother who tells children how good they are. Or perhaps you could come up with a disposable car because it is affordable and easy to get rid of when you are bored with it.

After you have thought of a product, think up a slogan for marketing it (for example, "Fly the Friendly Skies," "Progress is Our Most Important Product," etc.). Then think of a way to advertise it. Write the copy you would use to describe it in a magazine or on a T.V. commercial; imagine what pictures you would use to get your message across.

In your head, try to "sell" the product to your lover. Does he want to buy it? Does he think it is valuable, too silly, too expensive, too superficial, etc.?

If you were your lover, would you consider buying it? If not, why not? If you were to consider buying it, of what value would it be to you?

Here is the most difficult part of the exercise. Remembering Exercise 2, become the product you created. Describe yourself, pointing out the features, advantages and benefits. Example: 'I am a disposable automobile. I am small and good looking. I give you good service for a period of one year, and then you can throw me away. I'll never become boring to you, and I'll never cost more than you can afford.'

Now, pretend you are your lover, and you have just been offered the product. Truthfully respond as to whether the product is worth buying. Example: 'I (as your lover) will not buy you because I'm looking for a class automobile that will last a lifetime. At times I might become bored, but it is worth a little boredom to have an automobile that is reliable.'"

Although I generally reserve this particular exercise for group workshops, it can be an extremely powerful tool when used properly with couples "at the crossroad." I handed Ann and Mike each a sheet of paper to record their responses and, after precisely six minutes (two minutes for each task), I asked them to sit comfortably facing each other. Their job, I suggested, was to share the results as truthfully as possible.

Ann's response: "My product is a new kind of rifle that shoots 'relaxation' rays that won't hurt anybody, but would make them sit down and talk instead. The slogan would be something like, 'Kill 'em with kindness.' The product would be advertised in all men's magazines. The copy would say something like, 'Kill your enemy with kindness and never be angry/frightened again.'"

Mike's response: "I took a different approach to the exercise. My product was more practical, I guess. My product is an anti-virus program that works on people rather than computers. You plug some-one in and within minutes you know where the problems are, and the program repairs the fault automatically. Not only that, but it also builds a firewall against other possible hazards to your health. The slogan would be something like 'Make proper reparations perfectly. Buy HIAV—The Human Immuno Anti Virus.' I would advertise the product in medical magazines, health-related magazines, and in major news magazines."

I suggested that Ann become her product and "sell" herself to Mike. Apparently sensing it that it was going to be a difficult job, she took and deep breath and said, "I'm reliable and last forever. You can use me to make friends out of enemies. No more killing, no more harm. Use me and I'll faithfully protect you and your family."

The next part of the experiment was more difficult. I asked Mike to sit face to face with Ann and to let her know honestly whether she was worth "buying."

"Ann," he began, "I know you are the most reliable person in the world, but I can't buy you."

Ann was dumbstruck. I could see her shrivel up inside.

"Let me tell you why I couldn't buy you," Mike continued. "Killing 'em with kindness just doesn't work in the real world. Turning the other cheek is hardly the approach any man worth his salt would use if his family were in trouble."

It looked like Mike might have bought some trouble with his comments. I was eager to see what he would say next and how Ann would respond.

When it was his turn to share his product with Ann, Mike said, "I am an AntiVirus that will protect you from health problems and repair you if an illness slips by. I last forever. Just plug me in and I will safeguard you."

Ann had pulled herself together by the time he had finished his statement. "I shall buy you on one condition."

Mike's ears perked up. Although he had rejected her product, she might buy his. "That would be wonderful," he said gratefully.

"Yes, I shall buy you and your product only if it can repair a broken heart." Ann was on the verge of tears. Mike had hurt her, but he realized—as did she—that all lasting relationships are built on truth and honesty. If he had "bought" Ann just to patronize her, she might have felt discounted and resentful.

Mike's response was immediate. "I am not designed to repair broken hearts, only to repair viral infections, but I think I can rewrite the program to include broken hearts as well."

"In that case," replied Ann, "I shall not only buy you, I shall also recalibrate myself—as a relaxation rifle—so that I can shoot real bullets just in case the 'Kill 'em with kindness' approach won't work."

Mike was so relieved that he actually clapped his hands. They both had been able to sell themselves— and without too much compromising at that!

The most important result of this exercise is a greater awareness of one's self-image. The product you have created really does represent a truth about you and your lover. If, in your view, your lover does not want to buy the product, there is a very good chance that your lover does not want to buy you in real life either. This, of course, is a fantasy exercise: it reveals how you see yourself. If you are doing this exercise by yourself, note how much selling you have to do in order to get your imagined lover to buy you. Better yet, do the exercise again together with your lover, and share your responses. You can learn more about each other during this five-minute exercise than you can during a month of dates. If it turns out that neither of you can "sell" your respective products, it may be time to start questioning the viability of the relationship.

Exercise 5—Finger Pointing

I introduced the Finger-Pointer Exercise with the following description:

"A common complaint we have about our lover is that he is so 'demanding.' The demands come out as finger-pointing words such as 'should,' 'ought to,' 'have to,' 'got to,' 'need to,' and 'must.' These words are generally designed to control people—through guilt, shame, or emotional bullying. The effects on people generally are the same: people end up feeling resentful and angry. The following exercise will help you get in touch with the quality of your partner's demands and expectations:

Find a comfortable place, settle in, and close your eyes. Imagine you are looking at yourself from above—from a vantage point that will reveal all your imperfections. See yourself sitting with your eyes closed. See what you are wearing; see your facial features, your clothing, and your posture. Imagine you have an x-ray machine that reveals your thoughts and feelings.

As you scan yourself, silently criticize what you see. Tell yourself what you should be doing or how you ought to behave in order to be accepted. Begin each sentence with 'You should…,' or 'You really ought to…,' or 'If you really want to be accepted, you must ….' Listen to your voice, to the quality of your speech, as you recite the long list of complaints and criticisms. Is your voice harsh or helpful? As you recite these criticisms, become aware of your body. How do you respond to criticism?

Now, pretend that the demanding voice is the voice of your lover. Answer each "should" sentence you listed above. For example, looking down on yourself, you-as-your-lover might say, 'You should lose weight.' Answer this "should" with an "I" statement such as, 'I hate it when you tell me what to do!' Become aware of the kinds of feelings that are aroused.

Consider the words you use to answer your lover's criticisms. Are they the same ones you use in real life?"

Ann's reaction was immediate and a bit frightening to Mike. "As I scanned myself," she told us, "the word 'foolish' kept popping up in my mind. I saw myself dressed casually, trying to write. The demanding voice said, 'If you really want me to accept you, you must cut out that foolishness. Get a real job. Take care of your chores here at home. You need to grow up. You need stop being so spoiled.' The voice just wouldn't stop badgering me. Come to think of it, that voice has badgered me for years!"

Mike became alarmed. "You don't mean to say that you think I'm badgering you or making demands." His head dropped to his chest.

"No, not you, Mike. The same voice seemed to belong to two different people, I think. It was my father's voice when he became angry with my mother, and it was my ex-husband's voice when he became angry with me. Both of them were constantly criticizing and telling us—my mother and me—what we should be doing."

Mike looked relieved and concerned at the same time. I suggested that Ann make a list of "should" statements and say them out loud. The task took only a second. The "shoulds" had been in her mind for years and years just ready to pop out.

"Ok," she said, "the critical voice says 'You should take better care of the house. You should stop writing and get a part-time job to help pay the bills. You should go to the gym and do aerobics.'"

"And what do you say in response?"

"I feel like crying. I don't want to fight. I don't want to say what I'm really thinking. I loved my father and I loved my ex-husband when we first met. I don't want to tell them how I feel."

"But, Ann, if it somehow affects us, then you do have to confront those nasty voices." Mike was sitting next to her now, hand on her hand.

"Ok...I want to say to both of them, 'What right do you have to tell me—or my mother—what to do. I hate you when you say those things. I want you out of my life. I want to destroy you when you criticize me like that. You are a pompous elitist ass. I will write when and what I want to write. I will wear the clothes I want to wear. I will eat chocolate Sundays until I weigh a thousand pounds if I want to. I'll have no more shoulds or have-tos from you, or you're fired from my life." She suddenly became very quiet.

Mike, brave soul that he was, tried to break her mood with humor. "Ann, dear," he said, "I love when you are so direct. But, really, don't you think you should have said it a long time ago?"

"Should!" she responded through gritted teeth. Ann was ready to pounce on him...until...until she took a closer look at the man she loved, and found that he was smiling. Her anger melted and she held his hand more tightly.

Mike's experience was no less profound. As he scanned his body, he heard the critical voice clearly and sharply say, "If you want me to accept you, you have to be a man! Straighten out those shoulders. Think, think, think! Big boys don't cry." The voice was relentless.

Every time Mike heard the voice, he winced as though each word and each demand had a pointy barb that dug into his flesh.

When I asked him to respond to the voice, he nearly screamed, "I don't have to listen to you anymore. You're dead!" Tears formed in the corners of his eyes as he explained that the voice belonged not to his father, but rather to his mother! While his father had apparently established the rule that logic and manliness excluded emotions, it was his mother who seemed to enforce the rule of the house. This was confusing to him. At a conscious level he did not remember her behaving in that way. He remembered only the sweetness and the support.

Mike didn't remember how his mother reacted to his temperament and to his early demands for attention. Nor should he have remembered since he was only toddler. By the time he entered school, he had learned the lesson very well: He kept his mouth shut, his ears open, and let the voice of the critical parent control his emotions. When I asked what he might do to rid himself of the voice, Mike's response was, "Nothing at all. My mother was a wonderful woman. She got her voice from her mother and from my father, and she passed it down to me. Now that I'm aware of it, I need to be responsible for my actions and my feelings. My mother's not here, my father's not here, and it's time for me to return their critical voices to the grave. I still love them. They nourished me with good training, good genes, and enough intelligence to make life relatively easy for me. But I need to throw out some of the bad voices before they ruin the happiness I've found here with Ann."

Exercise 6—Yes/No

The following week, I introduced Exercise #6 with the following instructions:

The past always seems to be with us. Memories invade our consciousness like uninvited guests. Nonetheless, it is important to remember that these memories are always imperfect recordings of past events. They are merely images and thoughts, not the events themselves.

Memories are useful to us because they contain clues to some unfinished business we need to complete before we can relegate it to the trash heap. This is especially true of bad memories and nightmares.

Helping you finish a bit of unfinished business is the objective of the following exercise. It is a particularly important exercise because learning to complete thoughts, actions, and feelings is an absolutely essential ingredient in a healthy relationship.

Find a comfortable position. Lie back with your eyes closed. Direct your attention to your inner world, the world bodily sensations. Focus on your breathing. Recalling what you have learned in Chapter 2 (Intimacy), inhale for four seconds, pause for four seconds, exhale for four seconds, and pause for four seconds. Continue this pattern of breathing until your mind begins to wander.

Remember a time when you were with your lover, a time when you said "Yes," but you really wanted to say "No." Visualize the event vividly; see it as though it were happening right here, right now. How are you dressed? Where are you? Notice anybody who might be in the area. Develop a clear picture of the surroundings.

Now turn your attention to the precise moment when you said "Yes." What does your voice sound like? Is it submissive, frightened, angry, aggressive? Say "Yes" again in the same way you said it before. Become aware of any discomfort or tension.

What do you avoid by agreeing to do something you don't want to do? What do you gain? Go back to the moment just before you said "Yes." This time, say "No." Do you notice any change in your breathing, any hesitations, any tensions? Keep repeating the word "No" until you feel as though your lover has really heard you and understands what you mean. Create a dialogue in your mind. Tell your lover why you need to say "Yes" when he demands something from you. Tell him why you are afraid to be honest with him.

Now, play the role of Mike (Ann). How do you experience being told "No?"

Continue the dialogue, switching roles after each response. When you become the other person, use your imagination to help you imitate his/her voice, body posture, and mannerisms. Notice how the two voices interact. Note any annoyance, arguing, resignation, cooperation, or fear. Finally, what do you think would happen if you, in real life, were to stop being a phony, and instead tell each other exactly how you feel? Take a few minutes to absorb what you have experienced. Then tell yourself a truth about your relationship. Use the first person, present tense, as though your lover were here with you now. For example, one truth might be: "I always say, 'Yes' to you because I'm afraid you'll leave me (yell at me, think I'm stupid, etc.)."

Ann's response: "I don't ever remember feeling that I couldn't tell Mike 'No' about anything. We have a great relationship, an honest one. But I do remember when I was married to my first husband I said 'Yes' to virtually everything. And every time I said 'Yes' to things I didn't want to do, I would become physically ill—nauseated really— by the thought that I would go along with whatever he wanted me to do even though I knew better. Yet when I even thought of saying 'No' I became so frightened that he would turn away from me—leave me on my own—that I cowered in the corner for the five years of our marriage. I remember one time when he 'requested' that I stay home while he went to his college reunion. I of course said, 'OK.' What I really wanted to say was, 'You're my husband and my place is by your side.' I couldn't say that. I couldn't even think it. Every time I said 'No', I began to shake. I guess the truth of it is that I felt like the little girl my parents taught me I should always be. It wasn't until I went through a lot of therapy before I realized I can say 'No' any time I want without the world caving in on me."

Mike's response was different. "I don't remember saying 'Yes' too often actually. I seemed to always say 'No' but I acted 'Yes.' My mother would always tell me how stubborn I was, but the truth of the matter was that I could never behave contrary to my parents' wishes. When I did do what I really wanted to do, I felt so guilty about disappointing them that I spent days in my room by myself, being afraid to come out lest they reject me totally. If I could do it all over again, I would say to them, 'When I say 'No' I mean 'No' and I won't be bullied by you anymore. Being fair, I have to say my parents never bullied me at all. I bullied me, and I tried to bully them by threatening to reject them if they asked too much of me. That's my truth: I can be a bully and I don't like that part of me at all."

Mike's recollection struck a nerve. Ann told him, "Every once in a while, I see the bully side of you and I don't like it, but I accept it because I know you love me, and because—with all of your blustering—you are still the most kind and generous human I've ever known."

I selected this particular exercise because unfinished feelings and phoniness—emotional dishonesty—interfere with communication, spontaneity, and harmonious relationships. Participants often have much emotional energy invested in the event they choose to remember, and energy invested in a phony "Yes" can't be invested in other, more necessary activities. By re-experiencing the event clearly and totally in the present, by identifying with the parts of the situation they had chosen to avoid, Ann and Mike created an opportunity to become aware of the feelings and thoughts that needed to be finished in order to have peace of mind. With this awareness, they could then decide whether they wanted to keep the undigested memory or to regurgitate it and toss it away along with other emotional debris—a decidedly better solution in the long run.

The other important aspect of the exercise was that Ann and Mike could now appreciate more fully the "truth" that prevented them from being totally honest in their relationships. We comply with the demands of others for many reasons. Generally, these reasons have to do with wanting to be accepted, to be loved, or to avoid conflict. And there are any number of us who want to seduce others into believing we are "kind" or "nice." But always there is a price to pay. Sometimes it's worth it and sometimes it's not. The price for most of us is too dear: dishonesty, resentment, and ultimately self-contempt. But saying "No" to every provocation is not the answer. The oppositional person is just as trapped as the person who always yields. Again, it is a matter of balance. Balance, in this case, revolves around a consideration of the demands of the situation. The objective is to be neither master nor slave.

Exercise 7—Ought and Choose

As part of Exercise 7, I instructed as follows:

Responsibility in a relationship means response-ability, the ability to respond to the demands of the environment while at the same time considering your own personal needs. Avoiding responsibility for how we behave, how we think, and how we feel offers short-term relief but long-term pain. The pain derives from the confusion and anxiety we experience when our ability to respond with intimacy and truthfulness has been compromised.

Make a list of five things you "have to" do in order to maintain your relationship (e.g., "I always have to give in," "I always have to make love when I'm not in the mood," "I always have to pay the bills," etc.). In your mind, say each of the statements on your list three times, each time with more intensity. Appreciate how your voice sounds. Is the voice whiny, angry, irritated, or submissive?

Now go back to the list of "have to's" and substitute the words "choose to." Again, repeat each statement three times, each time becoming more involved, more intense. As you repeat each statement become aware of your bodily sensations, tensions, and feelings. Notice what happens when you change "have to" to "choose to." Most people report there are greater feelings of control—over the power to make choices, even unpleasant ones.

Ann's recollection of her list of "have to/choose to" statements created feelings of anger, sadness, and fear. At first she was reluctant to tell Mike, but with his reassurance she courageously produced the five statements:

- "I always have to be happy when I don't really feel that way."
- "I always have to nearly beg you to tell me what's on your mind."
- "I always have to think about how you'll feel if I don't say the right thing,"
- "I always have to give up my writing time to accommodate your talking time."
- "I always have to be gentle to avoid hurting your feelings."

Reciting each item on the list, Ann became increasingly more uncomfortable. Her breathing became labored. She perspired. Her eyes darted around the room in what appeared to be an attempt to avoid eye contact. Her voice quavered. And she finally became so nervous she refused to go on.

I asked her to now face Mike and tell him how she felt when she changed the words "have to" to "choose to." Her posture and facial expressions visibly changed. She appeared to be more confident. Her voice became stronger and her eye contact was sharp and focused.

- "I choose to be happy when I don't really feel like it because I know it pleases you. It's a small sacrifice for seeing you happy."
- "I choose to beg you to tell me what's on your mind because, although I know it bugs you, just getting any reaction from you is better than having to suffer the silence. I first noticed this when I was a little girl. I always seemed to need to know how my father was feeling, or rather how he was feeling toward me. He was always moody, and I never knew exactly what was going on inside him. It seems now that, as a little girl, I myself couldn't exist without acknowledgement by my father. I didn't seem to have as much trouble with my mother. She always recognized me and my accomplishments."

- "I choose to think about how you'll feel if I say the wrong thing. But I don't like it one bit! I want you to be pleased with me. I don't want to make waves and ruin the best thing that has ever happened to me, so I'm really careful, and I choose to be careful. It is draining though and I wish we could correct that somehow. I hope I'm not saying the wrong thing!" (Ann smiled at the irony of what she had revealed.)
- "I choose to give up my writing time to accommodate your talking time. Getting you to talk any time is a gift!"
- "I choose to be gentle so that I don't hurt your feelings. I like being gentle with you. I want you to secure and to know that I would never deliberately hurt you. Having to be gentle isn't always easy. As a matter of fact, it becomes burdensome at times, especially when I become angry with you for some reason. And it's always hard for me balance my need to let you know that I'm angry at my need—oops, my choice—to be gentle. Overall though I'm much happier and I think you're much happier when I can be soft and gentle."

Mike read his list of five items slowly and carefully. Even now he couldn't bring himself to say anything to displease Ann. I urged him to continue.

- "I always have to figure out what mood you're in."
- "I feel I always have to walk on eggshells so that I don't chance hurting your feelings."
- "I always have to pretend that I'm listening to you when I really want to read the newspaper."
- "I always have to go to your parents with you when I would much prefer to go to the theater or even go fishing with the boys (Ann's two sons by her first husband)."
- "I always have to say I'm sorry even though I don't think I've done anything wrong."

Asked to change "have to" to "choose to," Mike looked directly into Ann's eyes. He took a deep breath, smiled briefly, and told her:

- "I choose to figure out what mood you're in because I've learned how to deal with your mood swings and it just makes life easier for both of us."
- "I choose to walk on egg shells. It's pretty tedious most of the time and sometimes I resent it because it's so emotionally draining. But it does let you know that I love you and I'm willing to be sensitive to your needs. In the general scheme of things, it's a pretty small price to pay."
- "I choose to pretend to listen to you because I know you pretend to listen to me sometimes. It seems like we made some kind of deal months ago when we first began to see each other; I listen to you and you listen to me—out of affection and respect, if not always out of interest.
- "I choose to go to your parents with you because, although I like my alone time, I actually do enjoy talking with your father. Maybe what I should do is invite him to go fishing with me and leave you and your mother to shop or talk or gossip." (Ann nodded approvingly.)
- "I choose to say I'm sorry even though I don't think I've done anything wrong because I've learned that saying I'm sorry is really like saying, 'I love you.' You like to hear that and I like to say that, so why not?"

The session ended with a hug and a smile. What better ending could we have had?

When we "have to" do something, more often than not, we are merely playing Svengali with ourselves. We certainly do not "have to" remain in a relationship that is poorly suited to our temperament, our sense of what's right and what's wrong, or our priorities in life. We may "choose to" because the relationship offers companionship, security, or because the neighbors might talk. But we don't "have to" stay in the relationship—at least in most cases. The important thing is to appreciate how we often limit our options in life, and then blame our lover so that we can justify our lack of responsibility, that is, our lack of response-ability: the ability to respond to the real demands of our life circumstance.

Exercise 8—Fears and Wishes

Most of us walk around with emotional splinters that insinuate themselves into every aspect of our lives at home, at work, and at play. Sensitive to their stings, we hesitate to make full contact with the people around us. These emotional splinters create a phobic attitude that reactivates memories from an earlier time in our lives. Unless we can convert these fears into desires, we become slaves to the ogres and witches called self-doubt and insecurity.

I asked Mike and Ann to try the following exercise because I wanted them to (re)discover how fear can be turned into desire. The exercise is difficult because it requires participants to take full responsibility for their behaviors and their vulnerabilities no matter how alien these behaviors appear to be.

Find a comfortable position and close your eyes. Imagine a place about three inches behind your eyes in what you might consider the center of your mind. When you have found the place most comfortable for you, picture Mike (Ann). Now list five things about your partner you are afraid of, e.g., "I'm afraid you'll reject me," "I'm afraid you will find me unattractive," "I'm afraid I will embarrass you," etc.

I gave Mike and Ann ten minutes to think of a list of fears and then asked them to write them down.

Ann's list:
- I'm afraid you'll leave me for a younger woman.
- I'm afraid that you will forbid me to write.
- I'm afraid you'll think I'm a bad homemaker.
- I'm afraid you won't talk to me when I do something wrong.
- I'm afraid I'm not brainy enough for you.

Mike's list:

- I'm afraid I won't live up to your expectations.
- I'm afraid you will think I'm silly when I'm trying to be romantic.
- I'm afraid you will think I would be a poor father.
- I'm afraid you'll think I'm a clumsy lover.
- I'm afraid I won't be sensitive to your feelings.

Now go back to the list of five things. Substitute the words "wish" or "desire" for the word "afraid." As you repeat each sentence, list the reasons why your fears might, in fact, be wishes. For example, "I wish you would reject me, so I would have an excuse to (run away, stop working so hard, go out and have a drink)." Compare and appreciate the differences and similarities between your fears and your wishes. Listen carefully to your list of fears. Do you really sound frightened? Do you sometimes feel you are manipulating your lover with your insecurity? What do you avoid by maintaining the victim's position? What do you avoid by not expressing your wishes and desires?

Ann's responses:

- "I wish you would leave me for a younger woman. If you did, I wouldn't have to worry about your rejecting me when I get older and I lose my looks. At least I would know you had a reason for leaving and that you didn't just hate me or find me revolting.
- I wish you would forbid me to write. Sometimes I just get so tired having to produce chapter after chapter for my publisher. It would be a great relief if you could forbid me to write and let me spend more time with you and my children.
- I wish you would think I'm a bad housekeeper. That way, I wouldn't have to keep up the pretense that I like doing housework. I think it's drudgery—the ironing, washing the floors, making the bathrooms spic and span so that I can impress

people with a skill I really don't want. Why don't we just get a house cleaner to come in once a week to do that sort of stuff? My, oh my, I wonder why I never thought of it before!

- I wish you wouldn't talk to me when I do something wrong. I feel so guilty when things don't go well that I really don't want to look at you or talk to you. Why don't we make a pact? When I screw up, you give me a few hours to wind down and then you can tell me either that you're angry, or that you still love me, or both!

- I wish I weren't brainy enough for you. The truth is I think I'm pretty smart. But if I weren't, then I wouldn't be so intimidating. I just want to be soft and sweet and caring. But every once in a while the brain gets revved up and I can't stop myself from being smart! The best thing you can do is give me a big hug and a kiss and just tell me how beautiful you think I am even though I'm being a wise guy."

Mike's responses:

- "I wish I couldn't live up to your expectations. It's like your feeling about writing. I sometimes get exhausted trying to measure up. I don't even know what I'm measuring up against anymore. I just know I have to be on my best behavior. Dot the Is and cross the Ts. It's almost like living with my parents. I know you've never asked me to be this way, so I guess it's something in me that I have to conquer—or at least learn to live with.

- I wish you would think I'm silly when I'm trying to be romantic. Not that I want to be silly at all. I just want to be able to loosen up. Be goofy if I want to be. Hug you and love you if I want without having to feel that there's a proper way of doing things—even being romantic.

- I wish you would think I am a poor father. I don't feel comfortable with your children yet and I don't know how they feel about me. If you could convince them that I'm a complete ignoramus about fatherhood, it would be much easier for me and for them. We would all know what to expect. The truth is I love children and I think your kids are great. I'm sure I'm more than adequate at fatherhood, but it would be so much easier if I didn't have to go through this breaking-in period with your children and your entire family.

- I wish you'd think I'm a clumsy lover. If you did, I wouldn't have to worry about not pleasing you. You would just assume that I'm not very good at sex and adjust your expectations. Yipes! There I go with my expectations again! Actually, I love making love with you, but if you thought I were clumsier, you might become more assertive, and I think I would like that—at least on occasion.

- I wish I wouldn't be so sensitive to your feelings. I worry that I'll hurt you or make you sad or unhappy. I couldn't bear it if I did that. Sometimes I'm so sensitive to what you're feeling that I can actually feel the same thoughts and feelings myself. It gets in the way—not often but sometimes—because I can't tell you what I need to tell you in order to make necessary changes."

The "Fear/Wish" exercise revealed some of the more vexing thoughts Ann and Mike had. Not that any of the fears were in and of themselves very important, but together the fears had put pressure on the couple and made them feel uneasy. By confronting themselves with their own fears and converting them into wishes and desires, Ann and Mike gave themselves permission to be themselves, to demand the conditions that would make them happy with themselves and with each other. As it turned out, all of the fears were discussed fully and completely. The unfinished feelings that had lingered on—from childhood in several cases—were recognized and dealt with. As Mike pointed out, however, many of the feelings did not reflect trouble with the relationship per se. If they had, the fears, with the proper attention, could have been vanquished without difficulty. What made it hard for Ann and Mike were the voices of the critical parent that their minds couldn't let go.

There are legitimate instances when fear is the only appropriate response to a particular situation. The importance of the exercise, however, lies in our penchant for fooling others and ourselves by refusing to accept responsibility for what we really think and feel. "Fear" is often used as a tool to manipulate others into untenable positions. "Fear" might lead to submissiveness on our part and consequently bossy behavior or domination on our lover's part. Our lover's reaction then becomes a reason for us to withdraw from the relationship, to withhold affection or sexual contact, or to file for divorce. And all of this unpleasantness could be avoided by our being responsible for our fears and wishes.

The wish and the fear, as Freud pointed out, may be the same. It is the wise person who can discern the dis/advantages of acknowledging the two sides of the same mind.

Exercise 9—Make-A-Sandwich

The "Make-A-Sandwich" exercise, already mentioned in the Preface, is an extremely powerful, if somewhat offbeat, approach to self-awareness. I handed Ann and Mike paper and pencil and asked them to complete the following activity:

As part of your training in awareness, I want to suggest the following exercise. Imagine that Mike (Ann) is a ... sandwich. (I know it's silly but trust me on this one). What kind of sandwich would he be? Take a bite of the imaginary sandwich. How does it taste? Spicy? Bland? Fatty? Tough? Stringy? Sweet? _____

After you taste the sandwich, chew it slowly and swallow it carefully noting the various tastes and textures. How do you experience swallowing (e.g., does it go down easily, get stuck in your throat, feel satisfying, give you a too-full or too-empty feeling, etc.)? _____

Do you feel nourished and satisfied, or rather that there is something missing? _____

The exercise was wildly successful. Ann marveled at the kinds of images and sensations she conjured up while eating a "Mike sandwich." Mike oohed and aahhhed while making munching noises. They seemed to be enjoying the adventure.

Here's how Ann experienced the "Mike sandwich:"

"Well, to be honest, I thought the whole idea was bizarre. Then I became intrigued by the possibilities. The sandwich was wonderful. It tasted like roast beef, a bit on the rare side with a luscious au jus that dripped through the bread. It was so tender that it dissolved as soon as I bit through the bread. Yet, it had substance, and the taste was almost sweet and languished in my mouth. I found the whole experience sexy in a strange sort of way. Each bite lasted only a few seconds before I swallowed it. It went down easily and filled me completely. But I craved more. It really was exactly how I experience Mike in real life. Gentle and sweet and sexy and yet he is a man of substance."

Mike was more restrained in his descriptions; nonetheless, he also seemed to have a good time with the activity.

"My sandwich was presented beautifully on a crystal plate with slices of tomato on the side. I really couldn't recognize what it was made up of. I'm not sure it was meat, but I'm not sure it wasn't. I do know that it tasted wonderfully dainty and yet it was filling. The taste was so concentrated that a tiny bite left an explosion of taste in my mouth. The texture was not at all chewy. The taste of the 'Ann sandwich' was so powerfully concentrated, only a small amount was necessary to totally fill me up. The sweetness and daintiness and powerfulness all mixed together in my mouth created a sensation unlike any I've ever experienced before. And even though I haven't a clue what it was that I was eating, I know that I want more. And that is an exact picture of what Ann is! Powerful, mysterious, concentrated, intense, filling, and dainty. All the words describe her beautifully. The only thing I can add is that it also describes our relationship beautifully."

Moments of truth are often revealed in fantasies about lovers and partners. Only by acknowledging the powerful message that each truth delivers can we ensure the integrity of the relationship. In many ways, our fantasies and the truths they encapsulate are the true directors of the life script each of us has written many years ago. They tell us how to interpret the world beyond the skin boundary. They direct the cameras and the lighting of the inner world. And they reflect the attitudes, the picture-thoughts, and the feeling tones that enhance—or detract—from the act of coupling with our lover.

The Self-Systems

A discussion about the "Self-Systems" brought Ann and Mike to the point where they began to trust their relationship but not necessarily themselves. They had become aware of hidden truths that work hand in hand with our self-image and self-esteem.

Deep inside us lies a largely unknown but ubiquitous set of beliefs that serve as a backdrop for our decisions about our relationships. These attitudes and values are so deeply ingrained into our character structure that we often have little direct awareness of them or control over them. They act as the vitamins of the mind. Without them we cannot behave or think efficiently or realistically, yet most of us carry on our daily lives as though they weren't necessary at all.

Compatibility with our lover often reflects our compatibility with ourselves. And to be compatible with ourselves we need to develop a benevolent set of beliefs about who we are, and about our purpose in life. If these beliefs are self-destructive or self-defeating, there is a high probability that they will be destructive and defeating to our relationships as well.

Our belief patterns, especially our beliefs about ourselves, our motivations, our expectations for the future, our notions about the direction our lives will take, govern the most important and yet the most subtle aspects of relationships. It is easy for people to tell us, based on what they interpret when they see us with our partners, that we are "incompatible." What people can't see, however—and what we ourselves often can't see are the tiny cracks in our belief system, cracks revealing that the real problem in our relationships is not incompatibility with our partner or spouse, but rather our incompatibility with ourselves.

Self-Image/Self-Esteem

How we respond to the expectations of our lover is incontrovertibly linked to the picture/thoughts that make up our self-image(s) and our self-esteem. Clearly, if we feel competent, adequate, and beautiful inside, we respond to our lover's demands in a more joyous and forgiving manner. If we have doubts about our virility/femininity, or see ourselves as small and inferior, we respond to our lover's behavior and demands in a very different way.

Self-image refers to the way we see ourselves, the way we perceive ourselves inside our own minds. It is more complex than simple picture/thoughts because it involves something deeper. It involves us as sentient beings. It is based on how we view our body, our intelligence, our behavior, and our attitude toward the world outside the skin-boundary and the people who inhabit it.

Self-image is often confused with self-esteem. However, the two are very different. Each of us has many self-images. I can see myself as a good father, a bad mountain climber, and a better-than-average psychologist. Self-image is not an all-or-nothing deal. Our self-image differs according to the here-and-now situation in which we find ourselves.

Self-esteem is different. It is an assertion of our worth as human beings. It reflects a deep and pervasive decision we have made. It reflects a true feeling that we have just before we fall to sleep at night, when the darkness acts as a truth serum that doesn't allow us to lie to ourselves—at least not until the next morning, when our psychological defenses are working again to protect us from painful thoughts and feelings.

We either like ourselves and feel worthy, or we don't. Esteem (respect, honor, love, and devotion) for ourselves doesn't really change—no matter what role we play in our life script. We may be able to subdue or repress our doubts for a short while, but in the end, we will have to make a declaration about our worth.

Fortunately, the unconscious mind and the psychological defenses we learned when we were children protect us against the overwhelming anxiety that comes with the realization that we may not feel particularly worthy or meaningful in this world. When these defenses break down, however, we suffer from terrifying nightmares, nervousness, and insecurity.

Self-esteem, then, is of primary importance. Without it, we can make few changes; and the changes we do make will not be permanent. Our self-image and our self-esteem work in tandem to draw up a viable blueprint for the changes we want to make and how we want to make them.

How we think about ourselves today influences how we will behave in the future. If we have a poor self-image, and an equally short supply of self-esteem, our behavior in any given situation will reflect these picture / thoughts precisely. Self-confidence will be minimal; self-defeating behavior will dominate our relationships. Our involvement with our lover will drain us of energy and stamina. If we are predisposed to do so, we will drink more, abuse drugs more, eat more, or display more shoddy behavior.

Every war has its casualties. The Vietnam War was particularly brutal. The weapons used by all sides destroyed minds and bodies. Physicians at the Walter Reed Medical Center were called upon to perform an unusually high number of amputations. Many of their patients required extensive surgery.

Of interest to us here is that many men and women whose limbs had been amputated would experience pain and discomfort in the very same limbs that had been amputated weeks before! At night, these women might try to get out of bed only to discover they were legless. The body knew the limbs had been removed, but the self-image wouldn't accept the fact. The image of a whole person had endured even though the reality had changed. This phenomenon, common among amputees, is called "Phantom Limb Pain."

The importance is this: We all suffer from "phantom pains" of one kind or another. It occurs not only when limbs are removed but also when we experience emotional damage. Humiliation, embarrassment, and feelings of helplessness that all of us have experienced may no longer exist. Yet we behave as though they do. All of us have felt rejected, teased, and left out. We were too young and small to understand, but the memories linger. The events now are mere picture memories, but we walk around feeling the same feelings of rejection and isolation we felt many years before. These experiences have been etched into our unconscious minds until we have lost sight of what's real: we are reacting to past life events as though they are a present reality. In short, our self-image and our self-esteem are impaired.

Can you imagine how this affects our relationships? We bring a troubling past into a relationship where it plays no useful role. Psychoanalysts call this phenomenon "transference." Most of us are unaware of the transference phenomenon; yet it is there, evoking behaviors that disrupt the smooth flow of caring for our lover.

Optimism

Most of us have early memories that enhance an optimistic attitude: the first time we walked independently, the first time we rode a bicycle without falling, and, most importantly, the discovery (for most of us) that Mother/Father will always return. The belief in our capacity to grow, to become competent, and to be loved lies at the center of our ability to face the future with relative security. However, if we fail to develop feelings that we are adequate and loved, our anxieties about life come to the foreground, and we create catastrophic expectations. Catastrophic expectations are expectations of destruction based on Phantom Pains we have continued to experience.

Whatever we believe becomes a self-fulfilling prophecy. Negative expectations beget negative life events; positive expectations beget positive life events. If we incorporate pessimism into our self-image, our repertoire of emotions shrinks: feelings of failure, worthlessness, low self-esteem, and inadequacy diminish our *joie de vivre*. Simple chores become burdensome; simple problems become unsolvable. When we experience a harmony within ourselves, we generally experience a harmony within our relationships. The question is this: if a negative self-expectation attracts negative life events, and our relationship with our lover becomes a "negative life event," whom or what do we blame? Do we blame ourselves, our lover, or the notion that "things just didn't turn out?"

The importance of the question is felt most acutely when we try to remedy the situation. If we can appreciate our own pessimistic beliefs, we might want to enter into psychotherapy before terminating our relationship. If we choose to blame our lover for the difficulty with the relationship, we might insist that he enter into psychotherapy, join a couples therapy group, or, more harshly, throw him/her out of our life without offering an opportunity for appeal.

If, on the other hand, we deny that there was any human involvement in the breakdown of the relationship, we might then go along blissfully ignorant of the terribly destructive role our own negative expectations play in our relationships. Our ignorance will virtually guarantee that one "incompatible" relationship will follow another until we run out of energy and—even worse—until we run out of dreams.

Self-Control

The theme of the chapter on Intimacy was contact boundaries. Self-control in many ways reflects our success with establishing those boundaries because it involves an appreciation of the difference between our inner world and our outer world. The world inside us consists of our feelings, senses, and behaviors; the world outside consists of people, the environment, and the "objective" experiences people share. We are self-controlled when we have learned how to assume responsibility for the experiences—behaviors, feelings, and sensations—that actually belong to us.

Our awareness of this phenomenon determines to a large degree whether or not we are successful in personal relationships. People who allow external pressures to get to them, who give up when adversity strikes, who, in short, let things "happen to them," lose self-control, and become victims of other-control.

Our self-control lies largely in our having the power to hire and to fire the other actors in our life play, and in our ability to populate our world with whomever we choose. We can fill it with ogres and witches, or we can find the people with whom we can harmonize. What we decide to do, of course, depends on our willingness to set the boundaries, and to make a clear statement about what we want and what we need as sentient beings.

Achieving self-control in relationships often means making not-so-easy changes, changes that require a rethinking of who we are, and what we want out of life: changes in attitude, in behavior, and in the values we have carried around with us for many years. The alternative to our changing ourselves is allowing others to change us. We can, for example, let our parents change us, or we can leave that responsibility to astrologists, to psychologists, to religious leaders, or even to our lover.

Most important to consider here is the responsibility we assume for our behavior. If we let others assume the responsibility for us, we can be free of blame if anything goes wrong. The price we pay, however, may be too steep: we lose self-control—the control to direct our lives as we see fit. We end up feeling victimized and cheated of our independence. Ultimately we may begin to feel like phonies. Nothing is real—neither our successes, nor our failures. And since we can't assume responsibility for them, we end up feeling unreal, too. And that, indeed, is a bad feeling to carry around.

There was a time when most of us didn't worry about who was in control of whom. We were mere toddlers, but we knew innately that we had the potential for growth and learning. We were young explorers who stumbled and fell, and then got up and tried again and again to walk, run, talk, and ride our bicycles.

Once we are able to accept the fact that awkwardness and frustration are part of growing, we will we be able to give up the idea that the stars and planets (parents, psychologists, and lovers) determine our fates. We will be able to respond to our own needs and assume self -control.

Self-Motivation

Optimism says, "Something good is waiting to happen." Self-motivation is far more assertive: it demands that we make things happen. It is an inner drive that insists we accomplish exactly what we want to accomplish. It is a commitment to persist and to persevere no matter how discouraged we become.

Dominant thoughts—and their accompanying fantasies—move us in their direction just as surely as the wind moves a sailboat along its path. If these dominant thoughts are positive, they move us in a positive direction. If these dominant thoughts are negative, they move us in a negative direction. Positive, in this case, means healthy, growth-producing, and empowering. Negative, on the other hand, means unhealthy, stunting, and dissipating. In short, without optimism and self-motivation, we cannot expect to recognize the "path with a heart."

Clearly, dominant thoughts dictate to a very large extent what the future holds for us (and for our lover). If we are constantly angry or disappointed in our relationships, our behavior reflects this attitude; if we are happy and grateful, our behavior will reflect this attitude precisely.

Self-motivation wasn't a problem when we were children; it simply was. "I'm going to make something happen" wasn't a chore. It was a fact of life. Our desire to grow overcame the fear of falling or failing.

For most of us, it was a time when learning was the natural state of the mind. Research suggests that creativity and spontaneity are reduced by 50percent between the ages of four and seven. As soon as we enter school, the researchers tell us, we begin to lose our curiosity and vibrancy. Perhaps this is essential. After all, social training and education are necessary; and social training and education require that we settle down, sit in our seats, color within the lines, inhibit our impulses, put the reins on our demands, and adhere to a rigid time schedule.

The price we paid, however, for becoming "civilized" was our innocence, our honesty, and our authenticity. As soon as we were enrolled in school, we were, at the same time, beginning to spiral down the path of "followship," rather than fellowship, and of manipulation rather than directness. Clouds became simply clouds rather than lollipops and dancing elephants; running became a source of competition rather than an activity of growth and celebration; tying our shoelaces became a developmental milestone rather than a successful adaptation to the demands of the environment. Our spontaneous joy of being alive was already becoming hardened into a commitment to achieve.

As adults, we became increasingly aware of the possibilities. The possibilities of growth and expansion, however, become the background, and the fear of failure becomes the foreground. Self-motivation, in its essence, requires that we overcome our fears with the desire to again grow and to ripen as human beings.

The battle between desire and fear is continuous. Desire reminds us of the times when we accomplished major goals—walking, talking, counting to ten, reading our first paragraph without a mistake, and asking (successfully) for our first date.

Fear inhibits us and makes us want to avoid difficult situations. It reminds us of the bad times, times when we doubted our abilities and our adequacy as sentient beings. It tells us we are capable of pain and disappointment, and conversely, it stifles memories of pleasure.

Desire tells us we are able to become something better than what we are at the moment. It thrives on words like "can," "want," "patience," and "hard work," distilling goodness from adversity, telling us we can feel better, think better, and act better. Fortunately, for all but the most neglected and deprived of us, desire and self-motivation are alive and well and living inside us, waiting to be reawakened.

Personal Influence

Our decisions about our relationships are affected by what we have been taught about people in general and about our lover in particular. We were taught by the people with whom we spent the majority of our time. Everybody counts. Every person we let into our lives influences what we believe and how we behave. The clothes we wear, the cars we drive, the candidates for whom we vote, and the quality of our relationships are determined in large measure by the other actors in our life script.

Not all people are equally influential, and not all influences are equally healthy for us. One of the most onerous tasks is to learn to determine what people and what influences are the ones we want to accept. We can, all of us, exert at least some control over the kinds of people we will allow to influence us; and we can, to a large degree, have some control over the ways we are influenced.

An essential ingredient in making the necessary decisions is a clear understanding of what we want to accomplish, because what we want to accomplish will determine the kinds of people with whom we choose to associate. They are, after all, people who will make reaching our goals an easier task.

Self-System Exercises

After discussing the basics of the self-system with Ann and Mike, I asked them to complete the following exercises:

List any "Phantom Pains" resulting from early experiences that may interfere with your relationship with Mike (Ann). For example, if you were teased as a youngster because of your weight—appearance, speech, compulsions—how do these memories affect you?

Ann's response:

"Looking back to my childhood, I can see where I might have a lot of the 'Phantom Pain' we talked about. For example, I can remember my mother always doing things for me. I don't think I ever made a bed or darned a sock. She always seemed to look at me as though I were disabled—or at least as though I was incompetent. I'm sure she thought she was doing what she felt was best, but it left a scar. I still catch myself even after all of these years wondering whether I can really do things for myself or whether I'm some kind of imposter who's getting away with something. It's really a stupid thought. I've borne children, raised a family, paid my bills, and published three best-selling books! And I still wonder whether any of it is real or whether my mother was right. As far as its influence on our relationship, I think it has very definite effects—all bad. I keep wondering whether Mike will wake up next to me one morning and see the thing I grew up believing I was—an incompetent, ditzy blonde. It puts me on my guard and it makes me resentful. Poor Mike doesn't even realize what I'm angry about most of the time. He just shrugs and lets the emotional storm pass. The worst part of it is that there really isn't anything he can do about it, even if he did know what I was upset about. It's a no-win situation for him. If he says, 'Don't worry about it...I'm here for you...let me take over some of the stress for you,' it makes me feel more incompetent. If he doesn't say any of those things, I begin to think that he's seeing through the façade and that he's ready to dump me. It's all very confusing."

Mike's response:

"I had no idea you felt like that! But you're right. I don't think there really is anything I can say or do to comfort you. Lord knows I've tried! (Ann laughs.) But just so you get it straight: I love you very much and it'll take more than a petty annoyance to drive me away. (Tears run freely from Ann's eyes.) Getting back to my 'Phantom Pains,' I've carried around the thought that I can't get close to people the way I would like to. The thought is like a splinter, it hurt so much. I've tried for years to get into groupie things, encounter groups, sensitivity training groups, and those kinds of group experiences, and I always walk away feeling emptier than I did before. I'm not sure where I got the 'empty' feeling. I think it may have been the emphasis both of my parents put on brainy activities. Instead of enjoying a day at the beach or picnicking or going fishing, we spent the day attending lectures or doing crossword puzzles. The message I got was that I was a self-contained human who didn't need anybody else. Certainly, it made sense. I know my parents adored me, but I don't think I could ever count on them to 'depend' on each other or me. Everyone just did his own thing, and I grew up with a fierce sense of self-sufficiency which even now interferes with my relationship with Ann. I think that's why I have such a low score on that intimacy scale we completed before. It's not for lack of love. It's more like a lack of getting outside my own thoughts. I guess the real irony is that I grew up exactly the way my parents wanted me to, and now I treat Ann the same way my father and mother treated each other." (Ann holds Mike's hand and squeezes gently.)

After the "Phantom Pain" exercise, we continued with the following brief exercise designed to clarify motivation and self-direction.

"List as many personal goals as you can think of in exactly two minutes. Next to each item on your list, indicate whether the goal will take one month, six months, one year, or five years to accomplish. To the right of each item, indicate whether your level of optimism and your self-image will allow you to reach each goal (rate your optimism: 1=very optimistic, 2=somewhat optimistic, 3= not very optimistic). Finally, how does Mike (Ann) help or hinder progress?"

Ann's responses:

- To write a successful novel—12 months—2 (somewhat optimistic)
- To settle down with Mike—2 years—1 (very optimistic)
- To enroll my eldest son in college—one year—1 (very optimistic)
- To lose 10 pounds—6 months—3 (not very optimistic)

"Mike really can't help me with my writing, except by doing what he's always done—letting me have me have my space and giving me a hug when I get discouraged. I've never really tried writing a full novel before and the prospect is daunting, but optimistic—sort of.

"Settling down with Mike is the most important of all my goals. That's really why we're here—so we can get help in understanding why two people who love each other as much as we do hesitate for even a minute. I think we're getting closer though and I expect that we'll be able to resolve whatever problems we might have sooner than we thought. (Ann looks expectantly at Mike, who returns her gaze with a small but approving smile.) I gave myself two years for that goal but I don't really think it's going to take that long.

"Getting my eldest son enrolled in a good college is another goal I have. I can't imagine he'll have any problem grade-wise, but I'll have to sell a lot of children's books to supplement any financial assistance we might qualify for. I'm optimistic about it. Mike told us he would help out if we wanted him to, and, although I might feel funny about it, I'll take him up on it if money becomes a problem. Education is very highly regarded in our family, and I would work three jobs if I had to just to make sure Jason gets a fair start in life.

"My last goal is losing ten pounds. But really I've had that partic-ular goal since my junior year in college, and I don't expect that I'll be any more successful this year than I was back then. Mike could help a lot by refusing to take me out to nice restaurants or bringing us beautiful desserts from the Italian bakery up the street. Y'know, I've changed my mind. Let's get rid of that goal. It's just too silly." (Ann smiles broadly, and Mike laughs).

Mike's responses:

- To get a job transfer to the United States so that I can be closer to Ann and the children—6 months—1 (very optimistic)
- To develop an interest in a hobby that Ann and I can share—2 years—1 (very optimistic)
- To join the staff of one of the local universities, either Boston College, MIT or Harvard, as an adjunct professor and teach a course in political history—2 years—2 (somewhat optimistic)
- To successfully complete the Boston Marathon—1 year—3 (not optimistic)
- To become part of Ann's family as husband and father to her two children—1 year—1 (very optimistic)

"Getting a job transfer to the United States won't be difficult. I've already discussed the matter with my supervisor who understands my situation completely. As a matter of fact, my company plans to open a branch office here in Boston and I have been asked to head it up, so I am totally optimistic about my future here.

"Finding a hobby to share with Ann won't be too difficult either. We both like golf, scuba diving, fly-fishing, and gardening. My objective is not so much to find a mutual interest but really to find time to share. It doesn't really matter what the activity is.

"Becoming part of the staff at one of the local universities will be difficult, I think, mostly because Boston produces so many bright minds and so many politically sophisticated people who know politicians who know the Dean or the Dean's wife or the Dean's cousin, etc. As I get the lay of the land, perhaps I'll learn how to charm someone with influence at one of the schools. It has been a lifelong dream of mine to engage really bright students in the political process. But I am not very optimistic at this point.

"Nor am I optimistic about running the Boston Marathon next year. The most I've ever run is about 15 kilometers and I don't train as much as I would need to in order to complete the 26-mile course. But, again, it has been a lifelong ambition to cross the finish line with someone out there to greet me with open arms.

"Speaking of which, my last goal is to join Ann's family. After listening to her answer before, I don't think we'll have too much trouble accomplishing that goal. I am so looking forward to a long and happy life for all of us. Her children are terrific, and I want to be part of their lives—not to say that their dad has been at all neglectful of them. Actually, I find him a rather interesting man, a bit on the stodgy side, but basically a man of goodwill. If all goes as planned, I would hope that Ann and I could marry within the year." (Ann is crying in earnest now that Mike has somehow managed to breach the barrier that has separated them for nearly a year.)

Hiring and Firing

I then gave Ann and Mike the next set of instructions:

Name two people you have "hired" to act in your life script whom you would now like to "fire" either because they don't handle their roles well or because they are uncooperative. How would the removal of these people influence your life? If you rid yourself of them, who will play their role (or did you decide that the role should be omitted from the play entirely)?

Ann's responses:

"My life script required that I work hard, never be angry, and try to emulate the virtues of some old-fashioned movie characters. Of course, I haven't been able to follow the script because I'm just not that perfect. But I do find myself lapsing into the role I seem to have identified with a long time ago, and I tried to hire 'actors and actresses' who were compatible with me. Many times, it works out, and some-times it doesn't. For example, I 'hired' Mike to be my partner and lover and that's working out better than I ever thought possible.

"A few of the people I allowed into my world, however, need to be exiled because the price I'm paying is too dear. One person is my girlfriend Kay. She's a wonderful woman, very talented and bright, but every time I see her, I feel drained of energy. She experienced some personal crises a number of years ago and still hasn't resolved any of them. When we were younger, she played the role of writing mentor, but now she just seems to want me to entertain her all the time. She doesn't work, she doesn't write, and she doesn't keep up her end of a conversation. I become annoyed with her and I feel tired after seeing her. This affects the amount of energy I have when I'm with Mike or with my children. I don't want to end our friendship, but I do need to limit the time I spend with her. I don't think that at this point I need a mentor anymore, so I don't think I need to replace her.

"The other person is my agent, Doris. She's been with me for years. At first, everything seemed to be OK. Doris was attentive and worked hard to get my writing published. I didn't mind paying her for her trouble. It was well worth it to be relieved of the burden of having to deal with the business end of things. Recently though, she has been preoccupied with other matters and with other clients. I understand that I'm not the only one in her stable of writers, but I don't think that means she can ignore my calls or my questions about her progress selling certain manuscripts. Before she became a successful agent, she was more like a friend I could depend on. Now she's—well, like an agent who's always looking at the bottom line, that is, money. I resent it and I think that she no longer serves me well as my protector or my spokesperson. There are times when I get off the phone with her that I feel so angry that it takes me a couple of hours to compose myself. That's a price I'm not willing to pay. I'm giving her the boot as soon as I can terminate our contract, and that should be about 30 days after I send her written notification. I will need to replace her. I have the names of several agents recommended by friends. It will be a great relief to finally rid myself of someone who is obstructing my professional growth because of her selfishness."

Mike's responses:

"I can think of two people who play major roles in my life and whose roles I would change without a moment's hesitation. The first is a colleague at work. When we first met, he was involved, ambitious, and a team player. Now that he has become successful, he has taken a path in another direction. Not that this is bad—not at all. But along the way, he seems to think nothing of manipulating his friends and colleagues, often with tragic consequences. It's got to the point where I look for ways to avoid him. If I could, I would just kick him out of my life completely. Unfortunately, he's now my supervisor and I can't simply fire him on the spot. He evaluates my work and reports directly to the president of the corporation. The good news is that when I finally transfer to the U.S., I'll be my own boss and I will report directly to the president. This is one case where I can remove a major player from my life script and not have to replace him.

"The other person who I need to deal with is my brother, Micah. He's become completely self-absorbed. He and his wife haven't slept together for years. Their children essentially raised themselves and now don't seem to have one iota of the common sense they'll need if they are to survive in society. Micah has always been very thoughtful and kind. Now he is so preoccupied with his personal crises that he can't function—at home or at work. He won't open himself up to anyone. He needs to rewrite his life script, and not include his wife in it. She's not a bad person, but the two are completely incompatible and it's torture to sit in the same room with them. The tension between them is thick enough to cut with a knife. I've tried to talk with Micah. I've offered to go to counseling. I've offered to take time off so we could take a long vacation and try to sort things out. He has refused every offer, and he refuses to recognize just how angry and depressed he is. I certainly don't want to terminate my relationship with him; he's too dear to me. But I do need to put some limits on the amount of time I spend with him, or I'll become as frustrated and depressed as he is. Again, fortunately, I'll be in the U.S. soon and I won't need to confront him directly about his behavior. Nonetheless, he is one of the actors in my life play that should spend less time on stage with me and more time with his children. I feel a bit guilty thinking these thoughts, but they are real, whether I feel guilty or not."

Effects of Influence

The following exercise was designed to demonstrate the influence that other people have on us—on our feelings, our thoughts, and our behavior:

Make a list of the three (more or less) people with whom you spend most of your time. Also indicate how many hours per week you spend with each one and how each of these people influences your behavior (for example, does the person influence your taste in clothing, recreational activities, sexual preference, ability to earn money, drinking habits, choices of dates, etc.).

State an objective you have vis à vis your relationship (e.g., getting married, being more/less demanding, achieving a higher social status, avoiding a less abusive relationship, developing a more harmonious relationship, etc.):

Indicate how each of the people you listed above brings you closer to your goal, or how they divert your attention from it.

Ann's response:

"When I'm not writing or spending time with my children or Mike, I spend a major portion of whatever free time I might have with two friends. One is my girlfriend, Carol, a fellow writer and a major source of support. The other person is my sister, Mary. I can't spend as much time as I would like with either of them, but the time I do spend with them is always valuable. My goals, as I mentioned before, include completing a new novel within the year. Carol has been enormously helpful in this area. She reads my work, makes intelligent critique, and offers ideas about changing thoughts, concepts, or words. I only spend about five hours a week with her. I wish I could triple it. Her insights help me enormously. She also seems to have an inexhaustible supply of professional manuals and books she is willing to loan me. And perhaps even more importantly, she urges me to go to conferences and to take courses. We go together; she supports me and I support her.

Mary serves as my voice of reason. She calms me when I begin to lose perspective. She prods me along when I become too lazy. And she gives me hugs when I become discouraged. She really is a terrific person, and a wonderful sister. I only spend a few hours a week with her and that time is spent mostly on the phone. The time is absolutely invaluable to me. She keeps me headed in the right direction, whether that's writing or losing weight or thinking through the financial complexities of sending a child to college."

Mike's response:

"At this point, I don't spend a lot of time with anyone except Ann. I don't like being around my brother although we were very close when we were younger. I don't like spending time with my colleagues at work. I've never really had the need for a 'best friend' because I've always considered myself totally self-sufficient. Nowadays, I'm feeling a bit cheated that I don't have the kinds of relationships with other people that Ann has with Carol and Mary. It's my fault, I know, but I do wish I could correct the situation. For example, maybe if I could hang around other runners I would be more optimistic about my plans to run the Boston Marathon. I guess one of the problems that we've uncovered is exactly that—that no one influences me except me. It seems to be difficult for me to give up control, and I guess that brings us right back to where we started: intimacy and emotional closeness are very hard for me."

The Four Alternatives

We have four alternatives when it comes to choosing people who can help us reach our goals: (1) we can continue to associate with them as we did before; (2) we can restrict the time spent with them;

(3) we can expand the number of hours we spend together; or (4) we can terminate the relationship with them completely.

Let us say, for example, that we have a friend named Jody. We spend approximately ten hours per week with her. She has a strong influence on us. She informs us about new social events that allow us to meet eligible wo/men. Unfortunately, Jody is always so depressed that she brings us down. Her influence is positive in that she serves as a clearinghouse for information, but overall, she exerts a negative influence because of her pessimism about meeting the right guy. Our goal, however, is to meet someone high on the social ladder. Given this information, should we increase our time with Jody, decrease it, or leave it intact? It is important to remember there are only 168 hours per week. Of this time, 56 hours are taken up with sleep and another 40-plus hours are spent at work and traveling to and from work. The remainder of our time is used to take care of everyday living. Are the ten hours we spend with Jody used wisely, or is there someone else who can help us accomplish our goals more easily?

The antidote for the unsatisfying relationships is not to abstain from developing social contacts. As Mike points out, this only leads to loneliness and a constant—albeit unconscious—craving for social stimulation and social structure which may or may not be expressed. What others often experience, however, is a person who is cold, aloof, or clingy.

Time spent with people in casual relationships is not time misspent, but it is important to recognize that major time spent on minor characters in our life script generally leads to minor results. As a rule of thumb, we should spend major time with major players and minor time with minor players.

CHAPTER 14
TO SLEEP PERCHANCE TO DREAM

"A leg."

The words belonged to a woman who called me two days before a dream seminar.

She continued, "What do you think? Or would you rather we wait until Thursday's dream workshop?"

I was too intrigued to wait.

"A leg?" I asked.

"Yes, that's right, Doc, I dreamt of a leg."

"And what was this leg doing?" I inquired.

"It wasn't doing anything. It was just a leg," the woman answered.

Now I was puzzled. What could a "leg" possibly mean?

The truth is we can go around and around looking for the "meaning" of dreams and possible symbolism. But sometimes—to paraphrase Freud—a leg is just a leg and to explore more exotic paths is not always productive.

Nonetheless, I persevered. "You dreamt about a 'leg.'"

"Yes, I think I might have been in the shower, and there was the leg."

"Would you please be the leg in the dream for a moment and tell me what you experience?"

"You want me to be the leg? OK, I'm the leg. No, no, I don't want to be that leg!"

"And why not? What do you experience?"

"I have psoriasis and I'm ugly and no man will ever want to be with me."

It turned out that the woman had a Saturday-night date with a new gentleman friend and she was distraught by the thought that her skin condition would turn him off. No matter how many showers she took, the fear that psoriasis would appear at an inopportune time took control of her thoughts.

I don't know what happened on her date, but the woman did show up at the dream workshop two days later. When I asked for a volunteer to share his/her dream, the woman raised her hand. "And what did you dream?" I asked.

Her response: "Two fingernails."

"Two fingernails?" I asked.

"Yes, and I can't decide on what color to paint them."

I felt like slapping my forehead with the palm of my hand. This time I didn't bother with the role-playing. Impulsively, I asked, "And which man do you want to kick out of your life."

She took a deep breath and finally said, "John. I'm dying of boredom!"

In this particular case, the dream represented a particular "existential" truth ("I'm dying of boredom"). In other cases, dreams do not.

Dreams serve many purposes, most of which are poorly understood. What we can say with some certainty, however, is that dreams and nightmares contain within them the seeds of truths that are powerful enough to change our thoughts, our feelings, and our relationships. So powerful are these nightly visitors that relationships can be created, sustained, or even destroyed by them.

Emily Bronte, English novelist, noted this about her dreams: "I've dreamt in my life dreams that have stayed with me ever after, and changed my ideas: they've gone through and through me, like wine through water, and altered the color of my mind."

"Man is a genius when he is dreaming," says Japanese filmmaker, Akira Kurosawa.

"Even sleepers are workers and collaborators in what goes on in the universe," wrote the Greek philosopher, Heraclitus.

In the 18th century, Lord Byron wrote:

Sleep hath its own world,
And a wide realm of wild reality
And dreams in their development have breath
And tears, and tortures, and a touch of joy

"Let us learn to dream, gentlemen, and then we may perhaps find the truth," wrote F.A. Keule, a German chemist who discovered the structure of the benzene molecule in one of his dreams.

And one more—an observation recorded in the 1800s by the English poet, Alfred Lord Tennyson: "Maybe the wildest of dreams are but the needful preludes of the truth."

Dreams

Dreams, first thought to provide the savage mind with the raw material needed to construct religious ideas, were taken seriously first by "primitives," later by the early Romans and Greeks, and then by artists and poets. Some "primitives" (most notably the Senoi natives of Malaysia) had always recognized how dreams influence behavior, and how dream sharing was an important part of developing a "felt-sense" of dream material. But it wasn't really until Freud in the late 1800s began to tinker with the possibilities of an "unconscious" mind that the import of dreams was finally realized by the industrialized world.

Each researcher and each clinician had his own view and that view generally came with a set of exercises designed to assist the dreamers accomplish certain goals. The brilliant psychoanalyst Alfred Adler was primarily concerned with the individual's ability to overcome feelings of inferiority. As a result, he prompted dreamers to use their dreams as a way to solve life problems. Phenomenologists, on the other hand, asked dreamers to enter their dreams and to describe the dream's minutest details without going beyond the information provided directly through the five senses. Many Gestalt therapists emphasized the need to "complete" unfinished feelings and worked with the personality fragmentation often found in dream material.

The contributions of dreamologists, cultural anthropologists, psychoanalysts, and developmental psychologists are all valuable. Whether we look at the "felt-sense" of dreams, the minute details of dreams, the existential messages and godliness of dreams, the universality of dream symbolism, or even the reflections of cultural ritual in dreams, we are left with the impression that dreams are a reservoir of pictures-thoughts-sensations that reveal our most intimate but unconscious awareness of the truths underlying the waking state.

The importance of dreams and nightmares in our daily life is unmistakable. They tell us things we don't want to hear. They force us to pay attention to aspects of our lives that are secret to our conscious minds.

Our particular interest in dreams and nightmares centers around their potential for revealing emotional and sexual conflicts, issues with life and/or death, and uncompleted feelings related to anger, fear, and love. In short, we are interested in them because they reveal "existential" truths that influence our thoughts, our beliefs, our decision-making, and our relationships,

Dreams as "Unfinished Business"

"Unfinished Business" in the sense that we're using it here refers to the biological and psychological need to bring closure to certain feelings and certain suppressed behaviors. Angry feelings demand that we redress the wrong—real or imagined—caused by other people or events. Sadness requires us to grieve for the lost object. Happiness doesn't feel right without a bounce in our step and a smile on our faces. All are examples of "unfinished business."

Most of us are not very aware of those kinds of feelings. They remain hidden because they are too dangerous to acknowledge. Little children, employees, spouses, and others engaged in the tricky business of getting along with people often can't voice their feelings or their thoughts because in their minds—and often in reality—the act would lead to abandonment, disapproval, or physical violence.

Among the feelings we need to "finish," the ones that seem to occupy most of our time and most of our energy include: sexual conflict, anger, sadness, failure, fear, and joy—the very same feelings that dictate our behavior toward our lovers (and most other people in our lives).

The best example of a dream as "unfinished business" came unexpectedly from a man locked up in the sex offender unit at a large prison in New Jersey. The man had been arrested over a dozen times since 1929 for "molesting" young girls. At the time of his most recent arrest, he was a successful caterer, the owner of three profitable carwash businesses, and the respected deacon of his church. (All of this despite the fact that he had scored within the mentally deficient range on psychological testing!). Examining his record, I found that the man, who often worked as a valet or butler for some of the more prosperous families in his community in Georgia, seemed to be drawn to blond-haired, blue-eyed girls about eight years old. In most cases, the girls were fond of him and came to regard him as a surrogate parent while their parents were away. He never physically harmed any of them, nor did he molest them in the usual sense, but he was compelled to stroke their arms or touch their hair.

I was eager to learn what unfinished business the man's compulsions represented. The man, called George, was also eager to discover why he got himself in trouble. A member of a therapy group, consisting of nine men, all convicted of sex crimes, George's hand shot up when I asked who wanted to "work."

I asked him to sit next to me. In front of him was an empty chair, a prop popularized by Gestalt therapists at that time. George volunteered the following dream:

"I was in a field with two girls. I was really young, maybe five years old. One girl asked me to touch the other one. I didn't want to do it, but she was bigger than me and I thought she would yell at me if I didn't. Then I woke up."

I asked George to tell us what he remembered about growing up. Here's what he said:

"My momma and me were living in a rich man's house in Georgia. This was a long time ago, back in the 20s. My momma cleaned the man's house and cooked for the family. The man had two daughters. One was eight years old and one was six years old. We played outside together all the time. Those were really happy times for me."

I asked George to describe the girls.

"The six-year-old—her name was Abigail—she was always playing and running around. She liked me and we liked to swim down by the creek. Everything was fun until she went to school. I stayed at the house and helped my momma. The other girl—her name was Dolly—she was eight years old. She was real pretty. Had blonde hair and pretty blue eyes. I really liked her. I think she really liked me too."

I asked George to pretend that the older girl, Dolly, was sitting in the empty chair directly in front of him. "Tell her what you just told us about her. Make believe she's right here with us now."

Without losing a beat, George began a dialogue with the blonde-haired girl he was so fond of.

"I miss you, Dolly. Remember when you and me and Abigail were in the field. You told me to touch Abigail. I didn't want to do it, but I didn't want you to get mad at me. I really wanted to touch you, not her. I liked the way you looked and the way you treated me and my momma so good back in those days. I've been searching for you all over. I keep looking for your hair and your pretty eyes. I keep thinking that I see you, but then you turn into someone else and the police arrest me. Can't we be together again?" (Becomes very sad and tearful.)

I asked George to create a dialogue between Dolly and himself.

As Dolly: "George, you know I like you. We had good times in Georgia, but I can't be with you anymore. I'm an old woman. I'm married. I have five children and seven grandchildren."

As George: "But I don't want you to leave me."

As Dolly: "I need to say goodbye, George. We're both too old. You're married and I'm married and we need to say goodbye."

As George (tearful): "Please, Dolly, can't you stay for a little while more?"

As Dolly: "Goodbye, George."

As George (crying): "Please don't leave."

As Dolly: "Goodbye, George."

As George (shoulders back, taking a deep breath, looking at the ghost of Dolly's memory sitting in the chair): "Goodbye, Dolly."

George's "unfinished business" with blond-haired, eight-year-old girls was now complete. After a forty-year search, he finally found the girl of his dreams, and he could finally let her go.

Dreams as Part of the Grieving Process

Grieving means "letting go," and "letting go" means that we experience great sadness, anger, and helplessness. The (impending) loss of a lover, a parent, a child, a job, or a movie hero/ine, leaves us feeling empty—a hard-to-describe feeling that most of us want to avoid. After all, "letting go" demands that we resign ourselves to a life without the person, and there are some relationships that we never want to change. Often our losses are accompanied by nightmares, which make our losses easier to manage by disguising them. Nonetheless, our sense of despair, sadness, and the emotional turbulence that often accompanies the "letting go" process lie just below the surface of our consciousness.

Jane was thirty-three years old when she joined a counseling group for volunteers at a drug rehabilitation center. The twelve members of the group were responsible for the hotline calls and follow-up services. On this particular evening, we were examining the nature of personal loss and how it affected our work with drug addicts.

Jane suggested that she had just gone through a separation from her husband of two years and offered the following dream fragment:

"I was in my old house, walking up the stairs to the second-floor bedroom. I noticed that the railing was missing..."

I asked her to imagine that she was in the house now, at the present moment, and to tell us what she was experiencing.

"I am very frightened. The house is old and empty, still attractive but old.

"I am all alone. There is no railing on the staircase and I'm afraid I'm going to fall down. That's all I can remember."

A part that's "missing" in our dreams is often found in another part of our lives. I asked Jane to tell the same dream fragment from the point of view of the missing railing.

"You can't see me because I'm not here anymore. You're frightened and you can't lean on me anymore." (Jane begins to sob.)

I asked her to become herself and to respond to the railing. "I'm scared. I need you. You always gave me strength. I could always count on you. I could always lean on you. Now you're gone. (Sobbing loudly.) That was the last thing I told my husband before we decided to split up. I guess I still can't accept it."

Another woman recently told me the following dream:

"I was real little. I was riding on the back of a puppy. She would carry me all over the house. She took care of me and was my best friend even though she growled a lot and liked to show me how sharp her teeth were. Then the scene changed. I was carrying the puppy, which was now an old dog, up a big hill. She still tried to growl but was really old and all that came out of her mouth were little yippy sounds. I woke up crying."

I asked the woman to describe the scene from the point of view of the dog using the present tense.

"I like to carry the little girl around on my back. I can be pretty grouchy but she likes me a lot and we have fun together. I like to show my teeth off. They're really sharp. I don't hurt anybody and I'm not really trying to scare the girl. She is laughing and pulling at my ears. I don't mind because I know she loves me.

"Now I am really old. I have no energy. I am weak. I can't see. I can't walk. The little girl is now a grown woman and instead of me carrying her around, she's carrying me up a hill. I must be quite a burden but she seems to still love me just as I love her so she doesn't mind too much. She is very sad. I wish I could make her happy."

I asked the woman to create a dialogue between her and the dog.

As the woman: "I wish you felt better. I want you to be happy. You seem to be so tired and sad nowadays. But I'll carry you just as you carried me and took care of me."

As the dog: "I am very old. I'm sorry you have to carry me. I don't want to be a burden to you. Perhaps if you just let me lie down and rest on the side of the hill, I'll feel better, and you won't have to carry me anymore."

As the woman: "I won't let you go. You are too precious to me. If I put you down you won't get up again…I just know it. I'll take care of you. Just hop in my arms and I'll carry you and we'll be together."

As the dog: "You can't take care of me anymore. It's time that you let me go, so you can find someone else to take care of. You need a husband and children. You must put me down and let me sleep." (Woman is crying as she says these words.)

The woman continued the dialogue until she was able—at least in fantasy—to put the dog down. We talked about the woman's life and what might be troubling her at that time.

"I think I understand my dream now. The dog is my grandmother. She raised me when I was very young. She taught me how to sew, how to cook and how to bake, and she made sure I took my piano lessons. She was tough. She barked just like the dog in my dream. She took care of me and loved me more than anyone else in this world, including my parents.

"Now my grandmother is old. She volunteered to go into a nursing home not too long ago. She didn't want to be a burden on anyone, she told us. I wanted to take care of her. I tried to persuade her that everything would be all right if she just wouldn't give up.

She said she wasn't giving up. She was just tired and needed to rest, and that it would be helpful if I would just visit just once in a while and not be a pest about it. I finally gave in. I see her on occasion and write to her as often as I can. But how can I say goodbye to the most wonderful woman in the world. I feel empty just thinking about it. (Woman sobs for ten minutes before regaining her composure.) I guess I need to let her go. It's unfair. She never let me go, but I need to let her go." (More tears and more sadness.)

Dreams as Existential Messages

Existential messages reflect our fears and wishes about life and death. They generally take the form of a statement describing the way we experience us within our world right here and right now. The messages are powerful reminders of our mortality—our weaknesses and our strengths.

A gentleman of sixty years was recuperating from mitral valve replacement surgery. The operation, although successful, required extensive surgical procedures. His chest had to be "cracked." His heart had to be pushed aside and repositioned. A major leg vein had to be removed and grafted to another blood vessel surrounding the heart muscle. Despite this, the gentleman claimed that he was regaining his strength and stamina and was very pleased with his progress.

His dream told a different story:

"I'm opening the front door to my house. I find myself in a room that looks like a large foyer. The room is bare. To the left of the foyer is another large room, also bare—except for a few wall decorations and a window treatment. Directly ahead there is another room slightly elevated. Just in front of this room however there is some old furniture. There is no wall between the front room and the middle room.

"I can see an old beat-up sofa and pillows with stuffing spilling out. There's all kinds of debris on the floor—bits of paper, empty soda cans, newspaper all balled up. There is also a naked toddler running around, laughing and having a good time. He appears to be oblivious to the mess in his diaper that has fallen down around his ankles.

"In the back and to the right, there is a room full of people—strangers to me. They are watching old movies on an ancient screen, using one of those eight-millimeter projectors. The people are also having a good time. There's lots of smoke and a good bit of drinking along with the merriment.

"I become very angry and I begin to shout, 'What's going on in my house? What's going on in my house?'

Then I woke up, and I realized what's going on in "my house." The dream actually summed up exactly what I had gone through and what I was going through. "My house was a mess. It was in shreds." The reason for my surgery, I was told several weeks before, was that my mitral valve was "shredded." I also had debris in my body—a staph infection, small blood clots that affected my vision, and bits of residue from the surgery itself. The dream's message was clear to me. The truth was that I was the house. I was the mess!"

"When I told my daughter about this dream, her response was elegant: 'Well, Dad, I guess you have to hire some people to clean up the house.'

"I replied, 'That's exactly why I'm here in the hospital. I've hired the best housecleaners (doctors) I could find'

The man's dream revealed the state of his health; it also revealed the state of his mind. Different parts of his personality were in conflict. The "owner" of the house was angry that there were intruders—microbes and illness—in his home and that his house was "shredded." Another part of him, represented by the toddler, was in a state of regressed oblivion. The people in the back room watching movies were the part of him that was entertaining (and being entertained by the) nurses, the hospital television, and all the "uninvited" guests who came to visit him.

I asked the man to create a dialogue among the different personality fragments. I suggested that he begin by retelling the dream from the point of view of the toddler.

"I am N___'s regressed self. He has just come into the house and seems to be mad that it's such a mess. In the back, bunches of people are having a good time. I don't know who they, but they seem to feel pretty comfortable talking and laughing. They're watching old-fashioned movies. I see them smoking and drinking. They seem nice enough, but I wonder who they are. All around me is trash. The old couch is torn and the pillow stuffing has been pulled out and thrown on the floor. N___'s pretty mad about the trash and all the strangers in the back. I am not at all concerned about that stuff—or what is socially acceptable. I want to play and jump, and drag all these old blankets around with me. My diaper is messy, my hands are all sticky and dirty, but I don't care."

In reaction to the toddler's voice, the gentleman responded:

"I want to get this place cleaned up. Pretty soon you'll be too old to act like an infant. It's easy for you to have that nonchalant attitude; you don't have to get out and make a living. Well, enjoy yourself now, because pretty you'll have to grow up and start taking care of yourself and your house."

In this brief encounter with himself, the gentleman reveals how angry he is with his illness. He needs to remain in the hospital, accepting orders from doctors, nurses, and the support staff. He feels young and helpless. He wants to straighten things out, get better, go back to work, and take care of business. In the meantime, the regressed part of him appears to really enjoy the freedom to be "messy." The carefree attitude is something that the adult part of the gentleman does not tolerate easily.

I then asked the gentleman to be the sofa—the part of him that feels "shredded":

"I am the sofa. I'm not much to look at, but I'm still functional. The man who just walked through the front door will make sure that I get fixed someday, but right now I'm just feeling old and worn out. All around me people are having a good time. The people in the back room are enjoying a movie, good drinks, and chatting with each other. I hear a lot of laughing. The toddler is running all around. He's naked...doesn't have a care in the world. I wonder what it would be like to feel that."

As the toddler (to the sofa):

"Don't feel too bad. Things will change in time. The man will fix you and you'll feel better. And I'll have to grow up and I won't be able to be so carefree. All things change with time." (Notice how the tone of the toddler's language has already changed.)

As the gentleman responding to the sofa and the toddler:

"I guess I was hasty. I'm not angry anymore. I'll fix you (sofa) and I'll change your diaper (toddler) until you become more self-sufficient. I guess I have to accept you the way you are until I get my strength back. But what about those people in the back? Who are they?"

Gentleman to the people in the back room:

"Who are you and how did you get in here? I hear you laughing and having a great time."

People collectively to the gentleman:

"Come back here and join us. We'll wait for you. We have all the old movies you like. You can have a couple of beers if the doctor says it's ok, and you can make new friends. We're your past and your future. We live inside you the same way the sofa and the toddler live inside you. Don't be too angry with us."

As the gentleman responding to the people:

"Well, I don't like the way you just seemed to show up, having a good time without me. I'm feeling pretty miserable and I don't need any reminders of how things ought to be."

People to gentleman:

"Yes, we are reminders. This is what's waiting for you as soon as you get better. Be patient, sit it out for a few weeks and then come to visit. We'll try to keep the noise down, but we're going to be here just waiting for you. We're really looking forward to it."

All of the parts of the man's personality demanded attention—demanded to be heard. Like puzzle pieces, fragments of thoughts and feelings finally fit together to make up a complete picture or a Gestalt. The toddler—the happily regressed part of the man—resigns himself to growing up; the sofa asks for and receives help with repairs; and the people in the back agree to be patient while the gentleman heals after his surgery. And because of this, the man can at last feel at peace with himself and with the world within him.

Ann's Dream and Mike's Journey into Intimacy

Dreams magnify what we feel and experience at an unconscious level. They are like boulders lying under the surface of the water in a river. You see signs of the boulders: the water parts slightly or forms a ripple, but the actual boulder is not perceived. By understanding the language of the river—by understanding the language of the dream—we begin to understand the basic needs, desires, fears, and angers that motivate our lovers and us. More importantly, we begin to realize how to resolve emotional conflicts that play havoc with our relationships.

Ann's and Mike's last session was devoted to dreams. I wanted to help them bring to a close whatever misgivings they might have about themselves, about their relationship, and about each other. This dream session, however, was different: I asked Ann and Mike to share the same dream. This is not a common approach to dream work, but, having used the approach in the past, I knew it was an effective way for them to communicate their emotional and physical needs. We began with a dream fragment offered by Ann. I asked her to tell the dream in the first person, present tense, and to help us feel as though we are really there in the dream with her:

"Mike and I are in bed together. He has his back toward me. I'm feeling hurt and angry. Why is he turning his back on me? He seems to be preoccupied with something else. I stroke his hair. Still he doesn't move. I pull him toward me, but he seems to want no part of me. I am confused. What have I done wrong? What have I done wrong? I wake up crying (Ann begins to cry)."

I asked Ann to create an ending for the dream:

"I have to wake up. It is too painful for me to feel this rejection from the man I love."

I repeat the request:

"Ok. Here goes. Mike turns away from me and I'm feeling hurt. I say, 'What have I done wrong? How come you don't love me?' He doesn't answer me. I poke him. Answer me! Why don't you love me? He still doesn't answer me. I punch him on the back and on the shoulders. He doesn't move. Then I notice that he is shaking, sobbing really. I am feeling very sad. What is wrong, I ask him. Why aren't you talking to me? Why don't you love me? He continues to cry. He's not looking at me. He's turned over on his left side. I can't see his face. I want to see his face. I love him and I want to see his face."

I ask Ann to say this directly to Mike.

"I love you and I want to see your face. I don't want you to turn your back on me. I want to see your face. What have I done wrong? Why can't you love me the way I love you?"

Mike's response:

"But I do love you. I am listening to you and it breaks my heart that I can't show you the affection that you crave. I turn my back on you only because I don't want to see how sad you are. My mind and my body aches for you, and I don't know how to show it." (Tears)

I asked Mike to share Ann's dream, to enter it and to change the ending of the dream in any way he wants.

"I'm lying in bed with Ann. She snuggles up close to me, but my back is turned toward her. She wants me to hold her. I'm having trouble showing my affection. It makes me anxious to have someone that close to me emotionally. I never experienced that sort of thing growing up."

I point out that he is talking about the dream and not really experiencing it in the now. Again, I suggest that he can change the dream in any way he wants.

"OK. I'm lying next to Ann. She's pulling me closer. I turn over and face her. I see her eyes. I touch her face. I smell her hair. She is very beautiful. I say to her, 'Will you marry me? And she says...I don't know what she says."

I said, "Ask her now, Mike. Ask her what she wants to do."

Mike turned toward Ann. Her face brightened.

"Ann, darling, you know I love you. I can't always show it, but my affection for you and the children is real. I want to be with you for the rest of my life. Will you marry me?"

Ann pulled him closer. Looking straight into his eyes, she said, "Of course I'll marry you. It's all I've thought about for the past six months."

The session ended. After giving me a warm handshake and expressing their gratitude, Ann and Mike left the office, walking arm in arm. I next heard from them two months later. Inside the invitation to their wedding was a handwritten note signed by both of them. The note said, "Thanks for helping us find the 'path with a heart.'"

CHAPTER 15
THE BIG PICTURE

N ow that you have learned about the nature of love and compatibility, about intimacy and passion, about needs, fears, and desires, about lifestyles and life scripts, it's time to confront yourself with the truth about your relationship. In short, it's time for you to expose yourself to your most severe critic—yourself.

The "Big Picture" appears when you have tasted all the facets of your relationship and you have an insight: "This is the guy/gal I want to spend the rest of my life with," or less happily when you realize you "want no part of this guy/gal." Values, beliefs, caresses, thoughts, and feelings fuse, and hopefully you finally recognize whether the person you're with is a major player in your life script. The picture is there in front of you—on the big screen in Cinemascope, and in Dolby sound. You may have found someone who makes you feel beautiful and graceful inside, and who, more than anything else, enhances your humaness.

Unfortunately, the Big Picture is not always positive. You may have discovered that your lover is not the right person for you. You may have discovered knots and nausea instead of lightning bolts. You may have discovered feelings and thoughts that leave you with a sense of dread, or, even worse, a sense of deadness.

Developing the Big Picture helps you pull together the results of the exercises presented in previous chapters. With these results you will be able to look (semi-) objectively at the quality of your relationship with your lover and draw conclusions about what you have seen, what you have heard, and what you have felt.

It is important you recognize that your mind has been designed to entertain you in moments of boredom, and to excuse your poor judgments in moments of stress. All of us tend to rationalize, to repress, and to suppress behaviors—our lover's and our own—at certain times in order to maintain a sense of emotional equilibrium.

To help you be a bit more "objective," I want to offer the following brief scales that will help you weigh the factors essential to a more enlightened decision about your relationship with your lover.

After recording your responses, adding up the numbers, and studying the past performances of both you and your lover, you can make an educated guess about the viability of your relationship in the short run, and, perhaps, about the likelihood that it will last over the long haul.

The brief scales below summarize your readings and observations. They will reveal to you how compatible you are with your lover, whether you can tolerate differences in lifestyle and differences in motives. It will also reveal whether the differences in your respective value systems, personality traits, and emotionality can be accommodated without too much inconvenience. What it can't reveal is whether the relationship was "meant to be." "Meant to be" is a more spiritual judgment that falls outside the scope of this book and all others: it is made only with the aid of destiny.

Caution: these are exercises designed to identify contenders for your affection! The chances of picking someone with a winning combination of behaviors, moods, scripts and a fully functional self-system and lifestyle, change with each life circumstance. Each relationship is organic: it grows or wilts according to the whims of luck, your current situation, and time. As the relationship grows and deepens, so do the odds that your lover is the soul mate for whom you have been searching. As the relationship wilts, so do the odds that you will be happy with your lover in the future. The caution is this: no book, no psychologist, no mental health "expert" can—or should—tell you what *is* good for you. We can only tell you what *might* be good for you.

You make your own decisions. We, all of us, are only the sum total of our decisions. If we win, it is wonderful; if we don't, we have to decide whether we want to go on to another relationship or not. If we decide we want to visit another relationship, we again take our chances.

Simply complete the scales as indicated.

1. Note the overwhelming influences in your lover's life, that is, what "owns" him/her. Rate according to the following:

1 = balanced, well-adjusted, centered

2 = parents, societal expectations, job hobby, children

3 = medical/emotional problems

4 = alcohol/drugs/gambling, preoccupation with self-destruction

2. Rate the weight/burden carried by your lover during your courtship.

1 = mild stress

2 = burdened but manageable stress

3 = overburdened, barely manageable stress

4 = always in crisis, generally overwhelmed by stress

Note: "Stress" denotes any situation or condition thath taxes the mind/body: medical problems, financial concerns, unemployment, overwork, losses (death, job, family, incarceration), poor peer relationships, dramatic life changes, concerns about children, marital problems, addictions, etc. For example, a lover who has recently become unemployed, has no financial support, and who has a serious heart condition might properly be rated a "3," or depending on the seriousness of health problems or the amount of stress, perhaps even a "4."

The concept of "stress" is extremely important: people generally return to a pre-morbid level of functioning when stresses are lifted. If, however, the pre-morbid level of functioning is 4ish, then you can expect continued stress, crisis, and emotional pain. The matter becomes clearer as you go through the exercise of studying your lover's past performance in his relationships with parents, peers, and previous lovers. If the information you need to make a decision is lacking, you might end up playing a longer shot then you had planned.

3. Note whether your lover was trained by his/her Nurturant parent/ caretaker, by a critical parent/caretaker, or by a generally impersonal environment, that is, the "streets," "gangs," or perhaps a foundling/ foster home of poor quality. Use the following rating scale:
    1 = nurturant, affectionate parents/caretakers
    2 = critical, cold, unresponsive parents/caretakers
    3 = antisocial/gang environment
    4 = impersonal asocial environment

4. Note whether your lover has a history of a strong normal attachment to his/her parents or primary caretaker, or an abnormally close bonding that might interfere with other relationships. Also note whether the bonding is "weak" or nonexistent because of early death/ abandonment of parents or a lack of proper care as an infant. The ability to bond quickly and deeply is often indicated within the first few minutes of meeting someone. If you feel that the initial contact is strong, but fails to deepen with time, the chances are this will continue to be the pattern throughout the relationship. The capacity for strong attachments is essential for intimacy in a relationship; it is less essential for the high passion/low commitment/low intimacy love relationship.

    Rating the capacity for bonding, use the following scale:
    1 = strong "normal" capacity for bonding
    2 = strong but abnormal attachment
    3 = limited capacity for attachment
    4 = remains totally un-bonded

5. Note how many relationships your lover has started during the past five years—or as many as you can account for—and how many times your lover demonstrated the kind of commitment, intimacy, and passion essential, in your view, for an enduring relationship.

This is a difficult item to complete, but it is also an extremely valuable exercise. The fact is, in most cases, what your lover has done in the past will reflect what s/he will do in the future. Let's say, for example, you know of three prior relationships and in each instance your lover made his decision to terminate the relationship early. Let's further assume that your lover was a potential winner, but for various reasons he wasn't able to win (marry, cohabit, become an exclusive companion, etc.) because of completely rational reasons (e.g., lack of compatible lifestyles, too much stress, too little bonding). However, you and your lover have been in a relationship for six months; you are happy and your lover is, too. This may indicate that you have worked through many of the difficulties that plagued earlier relationships and are heading for the finish line, displaying the affection, intimacy, and commitment for which you both have been searching.

Use the following scale for measuring your partner's previous coupling experiences:

1 = your lover's past decisions make sense

2 = your lover could have married but terminated too soon

3 = your lover was overwhelmed by the relationship

4 = your lover would be overwhelmed by any relationship

6. Rapport: This is an important item, but one most of us fail to notice. A deepening of the relationship over time involves what is commonly called rapport. Previously, we talked about boundaries and the purposes they serve. Some people have boundaries that will allow us in; others have boundaries that keep us out; still others have boundaries that vary in their permeability. Ideally, we want a lover who will welcome us in when we want to make a strong contact, and who will allow us to leave when the contact becomes too strong or uncomfortable.

When intimacy is high and the bonding is optimal, there is a steady deepening of the relationship: we begin to resonate with our lover, we see things the same way, and we respond to humor in a similar fashion. Our lover is a welcome guest who knows when s/he should leave us alone, and who knows when we want her to stay close. During the hormonal "chemistry" phase of a relationship, the relationship actually is stagnant; lust is merely lust, after all (but please don't underestimate its value). With time and experience, however, the relationship—if it follows a more or less normal sequence—changes into an admixture of libidinal energy, plus intimacy, plus commitment. This change is the hallmark of a deepening of the relationship. Each week, each month, becomes a celebration of intimacy; we are able to go deeper into our lover until finally we are able to visit her/his soul. The soul is the place where intimacy, passion, and commitment merge into a single indistinguishable whole.

Rapport comprises the level of bonding we feel at various points within the relationship. We assess the way we feel at the very beginning, at three months, at six months, at one year, at five years, and at ten years. If the relationship continues to deepen after ten years, there is something very right about it. Please note, however, that just being together for an extended period of time does not mean much in and of itself; rapport means that the relationship deepens with time. If there is no deepening, you may need to reassess what the relationship between you and your lover is all about.

Judge the deepening of the relationship using the following scale:
1 = relationship continues to grow each day
2 = relationship grows slowly but perceptibly
3 = relationship is deep but has reached a static point
4 = relationship changes erratically
5 = relationship has fizzled but I'm too scared to move on

It is evident from this scale that time and the capacity for intimacy are two of the important variables in any relationship (in Western society). It is also evident that we all need to be aware of our own "emotional climate." Without this awareness, the exercises in this chapter and all other chapters are simply dust thrown in the wind.

7. P.I.C. ("PASSION/INTIMACY/COMMITMENT"): See earlier chapters to refresh your memory if necessary. Note how you and your lover match each other in terms of PIC. High Passion/High Intimacy/High Commitment couples should have no problem with this item. Low Passion/Low Intimacy/Low Commitment people also have little trouble with this item. Those in between, however, have much trouble. Remember that H = High, A = Average, and L = Low. P = Passion, I = Intimacy, and C = Commitment. For the purposes of this exercise, use the PIC profile based on your ratings on the 3-D Compatibility Scale.

> 1 = HP/HI/HC plus AP/AI/HC or HP/HI/AC=Good Chance of successful coupling
> 2 = HP/AI/HC plus AP/AI/HC or AP/HI/AC=Some sexual frustration, possible feelings of emotional distance and boredom, but a well-developed sense of loyalty and companionship
> 3 = AP/LI/AC plus LP/LI/HC or LP/HI/LC=Little passion, some sexual frustration, poorly developed sense of loyal and commitment
> 4 = LP/LI/LC plus LP/LI/AC or LP/LI/HC=Limited chance of successful coupling

8. Reasons for Getting Together: Review the chapter on the reasons why people are motivated to get together and record your observations according to the following:

> 1 = you both have the same reasons for being together
> 2 = you both generally agree on the motives for being together
> 3 = you both agree only slightly, or not at all

9. Social Climate: This refers to a basic personality style that pervades the relationship. Reread the material on emotional comfort zones. Remember that similarities breed stability, but they often have boredom as a side effect; too many differences produce excitement but often have emotional pain as a side effect. Also, consider the climate crazy-makers create in your life while thinking about the comfort zones.

Rate the emotional climate of your relationship according to the following scale:

1 = 80% to 100% of your lover's traits fall within your comfort zone (may be too hot!)

2 = 70% to 80% of your lover's traits fall within your comfort zone (warm?)

3 = 40% to 70% of your lover's traits fall within your comfort zone (comfortable?)

4 = 20% to 40% of your lover's traits fall within your comfort zone (chilly?)

5 = Fewer than 20% of your lover's traits fall within your comfort zone (freezing!)

10. Moods: Reread material on "mood chains" and determine how compatible your emotional life is with that of your partner. Obviously, if your partner remains in an angry state for extended periods of time and you cannot tolerate having someone angry with you, there will be pain ahead. Likewise, if your partner remains withdrawn or isolated for days on end and you are a vibrant, energetic, socially outgoing individual, the odds against perpetual happiness are going to be a bit higher than you might have first anticipated.

Rate according to the following scale:

1 = Emotional harmony 70% to 100% of the time

2 = Emotional harmony 40% to 70% of the time

3 = Emotional harmony less than 10% to 40% of the time

4 = Totally out of tune with each other

If either you or your lover are caught up in one of the more toxic mood chains—Failure, Humiliation, or Love Addiction—and you can't resolve the feelings, give yourself an arbitrary "4" on this exercise.

11. "SCRIPTS LOVERS LIVE": Review the material on life scripts. Some scripts are tragic; some are benevolent. All are based on the decisions made when we were very young, often before the age of speaking. Our lover's life script, however, tragic or benevolent though it may be, needs to mesh with our life script or the danger of unhappiness looms abundantly. Complete the exercises related to Life Scripts and rate your relationship with your lover according to the following scale:

    1 = Differences are tolerable

    2 = Don't know for sure

    3 = Differences are intolerable

12. "MOMENTS OF TRUTH": Check your responses to the exercises at the end of the chapter on the "Moments of Truth." If you have completed them conscientiously, these exercises will have given you insights beyond any that you might have gleaned from previous chapters. Remember: the scale for measuring the impact of these truths on your relationship with your lover is very subjective. Despite our attempts to devise these formulae for "objective" assessments, our intuitions are still the best barometers of happiness.

Use the following scale to rate your comfort level with your lover:

    1 = I continue to feel totally comfortable with and trust my lover

    2 = I feel somewhat comfortable with my lover

    3 = I feel no comfort with my lover

13. SELF-SYSTEM: The Self-System factor, while it is immensely important, depends on our ability to groom our own attitudes and outlook. If we cannot independently conjure up self-motivation, self-direction, and optimism, we cannot—under most circumstances—conjure up the kind of psychic energy we need for an enduring relationship. The factor is elusive. For us to succeed, the sounds of silence that make up our most powerful attitudes about ourselves and about our universe must lead us squarely to the goal—the desire to form a partnership with another sentient being. The question is whether we at our deepest level want the relationship to ripen.

Rate yourself according to the following scale:

1 = I wish more than anything that my lover and I were married/coupled

2 =I hope we get together but I'm not entirely sure it will happen

3 = I don't think I have enough energy to run this race

A Final Word

Loving is creative living, and the person in love is a person who creatively bridges the chasm between her and her lover. She creates harmonious separateness, a circumstance that enables two different people to behave as equals. This equality is the act of balancing and integrating interests, and caring for her lover in a way that ensures mutual abundance, as when Romeo says to Juliet "The more I give, the more I have."

The process of loving/living is made up of responsibility, care, respect, and knowledge. Responsibility is the ability to respond to our lover's needs and fears. Caring is the active and lively concern for our lover's spiritual growth. Respect is the appreciation of our lover's uniqueness. Knowledge is the full awareness that comes with intimacy, commitment, and passion.

All of us ascend from the early narcissism of infancy to the capacity for loving our parents, our neighbors, our community, and finally our lover. Each step along the way provides us with more freedom, and, ironically, with a greater willingness to become more captive! The constant process of maturing, of unfolding our capacity for love, is crucial for the evolution of man as a social being. It becomes equally crucial for our own evolution as celebrants of life.

This is not a book about couples therapy: there are many other books on the market that address that issue. We are only interested in three issues: why people get together, why they stay together, and why sometimes relationships fail.

By now, you have become intimately acquainted with your lover and with yourself as well. With each day, the kaleidoscope of your relationship turns slightly to reveal even more beauty, more intelligence, more compassion, and more optimism.

It is my deepest wish that during your journey through these pages, you have (re) discovered that your lover is the one who makes you happy now, and who will be there to make you happy in the future. Care, respect, knowledge, response-ability, and diligence on your part will increase the odds that the match is a good one. A nod to Providence wouldn't hurt at all.

ABOUT THE AUTHOR:

D r. Neal Wiseman received his doctorate from Rutgers University in 1972, established a clinical practice in Massachusetts, and shortly thereafter became the Director of Psychology at the Hampstead Hospital in New Hampshire. In *Living, Loving, Letting Go*, he draws on his 35 years of experience as a workshop leader and psychotherapist to offer us a comprehensive guide to a better understanding of the three dimensions of relationships: Intimacy, Commitment and Passion. Dr. Wiseman is the father of two grown children. He and his wife, Marcy, reside in South Florida where he continues to offer instruction in Gestalt Therapy and also provides a weekend boot camp for couples who wish to strengthen their relationship.

CPSIA information can be obtained
at www.ICGtesting.com
Printed in the USA
FSHW020711191119
64255FS